IS **PRISON**

REFORM

POSSIBLE ?

The Washington State Experience in the Sixties

by WILLIAM R. CONTE

The Committee of Six.

William S. Leckenby, *Chairman*
Former State Respresentative
President, Leckenby Foundation

Norman Chamberlain, DEd
Former Director, Pioneer Services

Fr. Gerald Desmond
St. Martin's College

W. Walter Menninger, M.D.
The Menniger Foundation

Senator Ray Moore
Washington State Legislature

Leonard Nord
The State of Washington
Former Director, Department Personnel

1990

UNIQUE PRESS □ TACOMA □ WASHINGTON

"The supreme aim of prison discipline is the reformation of criminals, not the infliction of vindictive suffering. In the prison laws of many of our states, there is a distinct recognition of this principle; and it is held by the wisest and most enlightened students of penitentiary science. That the majority of imprisoned criminals are susceptible to reformatory influences is the opinion of most competent prison officers..."

"...While few are reformed, the mass still leave the penitentiary as hardened and dangerous as when they entered; in many cases, more so. It is evident, therefore, that our aims and our methods need to be changed, so that practice shall conform to theory, and the process of public punishment be made, in fact as well as pretense, a process of reformation.[1]"

Transactions of the National Congress on Penitentiary and Reformatory Discipline, Cincinnati, Ohio, October 12-18, 1870.

TABLE OF CONTENTS

FOREWORD

Edward, my son, was about ten. I said to him, "How do you make friends?" He looked up with a smile and said, "Be friendly."

The question asked in the book title suggests the question, "Is it possible to do something within our prison process that will generate a more compatible attitude and behavior by women and men who will re-enter the community?" Is it reasonable to think we would have better results by "being friendly?"

Were you or I to imagine ourself in the role of a convicted person sentenced for several months or years, how would we respond to a friendly environment? How would we feel after six months or six years of captivity when we walk out on the streets again? Wouldn't we feel more friendly if we had been treated as a fellow human — rather than with distance and derision?

Back to reality, we know that the majority of people sentenced to our correctional institutions will re-enter the free world. It is crazy for us to allow those institutions to carry on with practices that border on abuse and intimidation. It is crazy because we can predict that people who are treated with abuse and intimidation will come back into society in bad shape. They'll be angry or scared or equipped to engage in some sort of violence. So what's the use of carrying on with mistreatment? It doesn't make good sense.

Why not be friendly?

I worked on this problem for a few years. I was a member of the House of Representatives and served on the committee that concerned itself with the corrections program. There I became acquainted with Dr. Conte, who directed the correctional process, and with the long-term perspective and planning that had led toward constructive programs for institutional residents. I was also aware of the careful judgment and control being practiced with regard to predictably violent residents.

I was there when we passed legislation leading to the merger of four major departments, including the one dealing with corrections. The projected improvements and efficiencies failed to materialize. Knee-jerk reactions followed. The Legislature could look back and say, "Why did we do it?" I have felt personally responsible for my own lack of foresight. I should have known better.

"Is Prison Reform Possible?" The title asks the question. The book reveals the vision and the journey. The answer lies in the minds and hearts of those who will try again.

I visited Denmark in 1971 to learn something about the Danish philosophy and methodology of treatment. I found that high security facilities were used for high risk offenders. Lower risk offenders were living in relatively milder surroundings, the degree of security being related to the degree of risk. I visited one prison with no walls, only fences to keep cattle from straying. There was a library, chapel, school rooms and instructors — all in all a low key and positive atmosphere. There was a lock-up for residents who had broken rules but only two people were being detained. People were being prepared to go back home as better qualified citizens.

Back to our state, we have evidence to predict that skilled and considerate treatment of offenders will pay off for all concerned. High risk offenders can be better controlled. People who have completed their terms of sentence will be better qualified to re-enter the free world. There would be fewer repeaters. Our communities would be safer. And our tax dollars would provide a far better return, i.e., it will pay us to be more friendly.

William S. Leckenby
    State Representative 31st District 1967-71
    State Representative 34th District 1973-79
    Leckenby Company:
        Founder, President, Board Chairman 1943-79
    Leckenby Foundation — President 1953-86

ABOUT THIS BOOK

The Department of Institutions, a human services agency of Washington State Government, was created by the Washington Legislature in 1953 and attended its responsibilities in mental health, mental retardation, juvenile delinquency, schools for the deaf and blind and veterans' housing until 1971 when these functions were taken over by the umbrella agency, the Department of Social and Health Services.

The Department of Institutions prided itself on its academic orientation, which approach was heralded by the statutory requirement that the director of the Department hold credentials in both experience and graduate study at the research level. Persons meeting the requirements for the position of director were nominated by the governor and confirmed by the Washington State Senate.

This book deals with a reform effort in adult corrections which was underway before the Department became a reality and continued throughout the 1960s during which time many new and exciting efforts were extended toward improving the quality of care and the effectiveness of service in the corrections field.

The material contained in this volume has been organized with two thoughts in mind. First, I hope to describe what our team of correctional devotees felt was essential in planning and implementing a progressive corrections program in the 1960s. In so doing, I present a text representing theoretical concepts and behavioral science approaches to offenders and their behavior.

Second, I seek to describe both irrational and understandable resistance to change in the field of adult corrections, a critical area of concern to the social scientist. I hope the historical notes included here will emphasize the what, why, and why not of the Reform Movement of the 1950s and 1960s.

Much attention and energy related to prison reform seemed to center on the Washington State Penitentiary in Walla Walla. Media attention also was directed more to that institution. This is not to suggest that the reforms took place only in that institution. They did not. The Walla Walla institution was the largest of the programs, was more crowded and was generally viewed as having the more difficult-to-manage population. And, perhaps more important, it was probably the most traditional in its restrictiveness and controls.

By comparison, the implementation of the programs of Reform at the Reformatory in Monroe was a more gradual process, resulting in a less dramatic reaction to them. At the Shelton institution, the changes were coincident with the unitization of the institution and were not singled out as subjects for debate.

However, even though the events taking place in the Walla Walla State Penitentiary were discussed more often, each of the four correctional programs (The State Penitentiary at Walla Walla, the Monroe Reformatory and the Corrections Centers at Shelton and Purdy) and their leadership were deeply involved in reform. Each shared in the problems of implementation and each was devoted to the skillful transition from the old to the new as long as it was possible to work constructively toward transforming prisons into therapeutic institutions.

Crime in the United States today is an horrendous social problem with which the general public has become deeply concerned. Unfortunately, and all too often, a prison experience in the life of an offender changes nothing or adds to his anger and misbehavior. The public can ill-afford to support an expensive prison system which either does nothing or makes things worse. Instead, it is in the public interest to make certain that while the offender is "off the streets" and in prison, he is at the same time offered the opportunity to make changes in his feelings and behavior. This calls for a treatment orientation instead of just a "lockup."

Prison reform is not coddling prisoners. Instead, it is an effort to deal positively with one small aspect of the crime problem and to add a measure of prevention against further offending. Prison reform is in the interest of all: the prisoner, the potential victim, and the public who deserves to get the most out of its investment in correctional endeavors.

◊◊◊◊◊

Documentation for this volume is comprehensive and includes minutes of meetings with superintendents and staff, planning documents, published and unpublished papers, union newspapers, copies of the constitutions for various resident organizations, minutes of residents' meetings and a wide range of clippings generated by the media. These papers are on permanent loan in the Washington Room, The Washington State Library, Olympia, Washington.

IN APPRECIATION

I want to express appreciation to my associates in the Prison Reform Movement. Many had been in the correctional field longer than I. Most were willing to try something new in spite of their skepticism. Some had opted for treatment rather than custody long before I could boast of being a Washingtonian. All were sincere in wanting to improve services.

The individuals of whom I speak were, for the most part, in the field and had day-to-day contact with the "keepers" and the "kept." Many had been caught up for years in the old way of doing things. Their work load was heavy and their responsibilities great. They were doing well what had been expected of them.

There are many more staff and residents who worked together on the Reforms than I can mention here. Suffice it to note that they represented every professional group and every level of the staff personnel classifications. Each demonstrated a profound sense of caring.

Although I cannot name them all, I do mention with respect the Superintendents of the corrections facilities, B.J. Rhay, Roger Maxwell, Robert Raines, Edna Goodrich and Associated Superintendent Robert Freeman. It is to this group that I dedicate this book, a recital of our efforts together. Their council was invaluable and their companionship ameliorated the loneliness of the Olympia scene.

William R. Conte (1921 –)
Biographic Sketch: p.169

Garrett Heyns (1891–1969)
Biographic Sketch: p.173

INTRODUCTION
General Reflections.

This year, the centennial anniversary of Washington State, is a good time to look back and review what has been done, why it worked or didn't work, and, hopefully, to consider how previous trials and errors may contribute to the future. Although I thoroughly enjoy writing about energies expended in the past, I am fully aware that the only real justification for this recital of earlier efforts in the field of corrections in Washington State is to more fully appreciate present problems and consider new and better ways of dealing with them.

The 1950s and 1960s were exciting years for Washington's state-operated agencies in mental health, retardation, juvenile and adult correctional services and parole, and a host of community-based operations. In that period, these programs were administered by the Department of Institutions, headed by a Director who was appointed by the Governor and whose qualifications for the position included graduate degrees that were clearly mandated in the law.

Among the many positive accomplishments during those two decades were the development of local residential facilities and intensive educational efforts within the institutions for the retarded. The state psychiatric hospitals became institutions offering therapy, with the result that warehousing of ill human beings came to an end, hospital stays were shortened and patient populations in all three of the fully accredited mental hospitals were greatly reduced. Schools for the blind and deaf were updated and upgraded, and their doors were opened to allow residents of those institutions to become community participants.

In the field of corrections — perhaps the most traditional in approach and by far the least responsive to public need — courageous innovations were tried. Most have persisted into the present, and others have been modified to meet changing needs. All had their role in furthering basic knowledge in the corrections field.

21

As a social scientist, I was very fortunate to enjoy the company of Garrett Heyns, educator and corrections expert, and to be appointed Director of the Department of Institutions when he retired from that post. This writing will reveal his impact, illustrate his administrative skills, and describe developments even after his departure that were, many times, the direct result of his inspiration.

In the spring of 1963, Garrett Heyns delivered a commencement address at the Maple Lane School for Girls (juvenile) in Grand Mound, Washington. Among the points he emphasized was his concern that we learn from the past. He said,

> It's a good thing to spend some time looking backward and remembering at what stage in our development we had hoped to arrive by this time; what things we had hoped to accomplish. Then, see if we fell short. If we did fall short, we should make plans to catch up. ... (This) applies to all people. There is nobody whose life is so successful that he can't spend some time thinking about how he can improve matters.[2]

This volume is concerned with looking back and remembering. It is written with the firm belief that it may contribute to the development of a better future.

As I reminisce about the responsibility for improving the program in Washington's prison system in the 1960s, I find myself rethinking some of the same old questions and reliving some of the old anxieties. It was not that I was unacquainted with the difficulties to be encountered. In my professional field — psychiatry — resistance to change is a significant problem encountered every day. Surely there could be nothing new for me on this score as I approached the challenge of helping convert Washington State correctional programs into effective endeavors dedicated to meeting the legislative mandate for rehabilitation of the offender and protection of the public.

Then, too, there was little to worry about from the general public. The citizen interest, verbalized repeatedly and manifest in legislative appropriations, clearly signaled that constructive changes in other state institutions had pleased the public, and suggested that there was a readiness for more. It was clear from reforms in the mental health field that Washington residents had become markedly sophisticated about mental illness and were willing to pay for better programs for its victims: the media sang the praises of the Department of Institutions when all three of the state hospitals were accredited by the Joint Commission on Accreditation of Hospitals. There was good reason to believe the public would be just as willing to learn about the legal offender, and to support improved treatment for this very difficult-to-understand and frequently hard-to-handle population.

My courage was further augmented by Governor Daniel J. Evans, who asked for changes in state operations in many areas. "Planning Washington for the Seventies" was his motto and the goal. Governor Evans was always ready to accept new ideas, and he called for legislative support in instances when it did not come spontaneously.

Still there was anxiety. What about the correctional staff? Would they be interested in new program developments?

I hoped so. After all, their careers, their livelihood and their sense of worth would be greatly enhanced if the traditional, warehousing prison of the past could become therapeutic and bad behavior could be turned into good.

This hope, unfortunately, was not to be universally realized. Some correctional institution personnel, including some of their leaders, were not excited about improving their work skills, and they were not enthusiastic about trying something new — even with their very long history of abject failure when pursuing traditional approaches. In time, resistance to prison reform permeated the corrections system throughout the state. The staff's resistance to change was easily mobilized, and it tended to grow as the realization struck home that reform meant change. At its core, this change required the development of respect for the humanity of the resident of the institution regardless of how bad the behavior that brought him to the institution may have been. Reform called for an accepting and tolerant attitude toward people who had misbehaved (though not toward their behavior). It required the recognition that the courts, rather than the staff, were responsible for handing out punishment. Accompanying reforms, there was the need for a whole new vocabulary. No longer would it be permissible for any staff person to address a resident of an institution in terms that depreciated that individual or questioned his ancestry, or to use language that was unbecoming an employee of the people of the state. Prison reform called for respect, compassion, and consideration of others — attitudes that prison employees had not previously been admonished to assume.

Some questioned the need to implement prison reform, and others openly resisted it. Some staff asked "Why?...we have always done it this (traditional) way...[and] these people [their charges] are animals, they don't understand anything other than what we give them." There were, of course, some easy answers to the question, "Why?" The candidates for treatment in corrections were human beings in need of help; and the taxpayer who paid the bill deserved to know that professional knowledge about behavior disorders and their treatment was recognized and was being utilized in services for offenders. Not to use that information would be a disservice to all involved.

I have noted the substantial public support for program changes and improvements in corrections during the 1960s. The reader must wonder how this was possible in the light of the more vindictive attitude toward the offender in the 1980s.

There are, no doubt, many reasons why attitudes have changed over time. The public is angry about crime — and understandably so. Crime rates have increased dramatically and knowledge of violent crimes has been expanded to include recognition of the sexual abuse of children and the advantage taken of the infirm and elderly.

In addition, the scarcity of tax dollars has heightened the sensitivity of the general public as to how its money is being spent. No state in the 1980s could boast of such well-nurtured treasuries that concerns over the dollar can be ignored. Whatever the causes may be, there now appears to be considerably less public interest in what goes on behind prison walls, while reducing expenditures has become a topic dear to the hearts of many.

In the 1980s a new focus had emerged. As the public has become increasingly unhappy about crime and those who perpetrate it, the interest in the victim has increased. Hopefully, in the concern for the victim, our society will not lose sight of the offender. Real progress will be attained only when we approach both the criminal and his victim with equal vigor.

The favorable public attitude in the 1960s and the abject failure of the traditional punitive corrections approach to changing behavior combined to allow a long overdue reformation in the care of Washington State prisoners beginning in the early 1950s. This book attempts to tell the story.

Why Prison Reform?

Garrett Heyns and I had many conversations on the general subject of "Why a prison reform movement?"

At first glance, the question of a reform program seemed to be inappropriate. Much progress had been made nationwide without anyone so much as mentioning the word "Reform." Work release programs had been adopted in a number of states, and there were numerous examples of improvements in housing for institutional residents and in their food services and health care. Also, while there was no doubt that abuse of prisoners was continuing, it was equally certain that such inexcusable behavior on the part of prison staff appeared to be diminishing. It had been some 15 years since Colorado warden Roy Best's spanking of "inmates" in the presence of their fellow residents had gained nationwide attention.

In Washington, there also had been many changes for the better. New structures were developed to replace old non-functional ones, food and clothing had improved and, best of all, high level administrative staff were saying that what had been called "Correctional Programming" over the years was not bringing about the desired results and there needed to be a change. With these positive developments, and even an occasional improved attitude expressed in favor of treatment over "warehousing," wasn't that enough? Couldn't one stand by and wait patiently for improvements to come about by the natural growth and development of staff and its leadership?

The 1953 riots in the state penitentiary and the reformatory at Monroe led to unbelievable destruction and anxiety in both institutions. The administration had responded appropriately the following year by mandating the development of "inmate" advisory councils in both institutions to promote good will and to enhance resident-staff communication. Councils have long been recognized as a good method for bringing about a better understanding of the prison administration and their problems while helping administrators sense the stress and strain of prison life. An advisory council was established in Monroe immediately after the riots in 1953 and finally became a reality in the state penitentiary at Walla Walla in 1956. Wasn't this sufficient to allow the leadership in the '60s to sit back with a "wait and see" attitude? Or was the two-year delay in implementation of the Department's directives at the Walla Walla institution significant in showing a deeper problem needing more attention?

Dr. Heyns and I were well aware of reform efforts in many areas over many years which had failed. Heyns' personal knowledge of such endeavors had led him to believe that haste and over-zealousness might have been responsible for some failures. We admitted that we were deeply involved and felt an abiding conviction that greater change was both possible and absolutely necessary. Were we likely to be guilty of rushing too quickly?

We had cause for concerns as we approached the issues. Heyns had seen the problems encountered in trying to change things in state government, and I was fully acquainted with resistance to change as a result of my own professional orientation.

Heyns intently studied the explanations given for the riots in 1953. He was advised that the staff clearly recalled the warning of the National Society of Penal Information made 20 years earlier criticizing the overcrowding at Walla Walla and the rigid and repressive discipline there. This had all been changed: activity was the rule and Institution Industries had put people to work, or so he was told. Many recited to him the National Society's conclusion that "the overcrowding, lack of

25

work, and monotonous regime cannot make good citizens. It is doubtful that it can even make good prisoners."[3]

Many correctional personnel vowed their agreement with this position and indicated it had been heeded.

But Director Heyns was skeptical. If the 1930 recommendations had really been implemented, why had the riots of 1953 occurred?

And why had there been so many other unhappy incidents in the prisons?

I, too, was skeptical. The residents of the prisons were angry and were not expressing themselves freely. While many complained about things that affected them tremendously, such as poor medical attention, frustration in maintaining contact with their families, bad food, inadequate law libraries to study their legal problems, and so on, only a few were courageous enough to complain about the abuse they experienced.

With the approaching retirement of Dr. Heyns, I became more involved, and had the opportunity to observe the incarcerated in the presence of their "keepers." I was convinced they felt degraded and dehumanized by their surroundings and longed to be recognized as human. Unfortunately, this recognition was not significantly forthcoming in either direct communications nor in more subtle exchanges with staff. There was no way the rigid and militaristic attitude of the prison environment could be interpreted as accepting of the individual as the human being he was. There seemed to be no understanding of the resident, the problems that individual may have had, or even of the behavior that brought him to the prison in the first place. Certainly there was little consideration given to how to elicit psychological changes in the individual that would prevent further criminal behavior.

As I studied Washington State correctional facilities in the '60s, I was repeatedly reminded that as parents we are successful in changing the behavior of our children when, as we punish them, we let them know they are loved and that they are members of the family. We may dislike our children's behavior and want to change it, but we do not deny our children membership in the family because of their wrongdoing. In my judgment, prisons of the day often denied the resident membership in the human race.

There was no formal decision to launch the Reform Movement. There probably was never any real question in our minds as to what direction the corrections program in Washington should take. The only consideration was *who* would do *what*, and *when*. Garrett Heyns made the only division of responsibility possible. He would continue to do what he had been doing: he would pursue his interest in

26

an improved personnel and business management system, he would take every opportunity to address the issue of humane treatment for those incarcerated, and he would ultimately build a new institution whose architecture and program would encompass the basic principles of sound rehabilitation and treatment for the offender.

Later, as my role expanded and I was destined to replace Dr. Heyns as Director of Institutions, I would develop training programs to convey these principles to staff and I would lead the effort to change procedures affecting staff and resident alike. Common sense suggested that proper recognition needed to be given to what had already been done to improve conditions in corrections, and to those who had brought it about. Our predecessors had moved the programs significantly ahead, utilizing existing manpower and resources to the best possible advantage. The Legislature, reflecting a socially conscious public attitude, had been supportive in appropriations and in the spirit in which they were provided. These were givens in a situation without which there would not have been a readiness for the next steps.

The continuing effort to improve the therapeutic character of the institutions needed a name to bring attention and interest to the work. The name ultimately emerging from common usage was simple and straightforward and in no way ambiguous. We referred to the project as "The Reform Movement." Anyone hearing it would immediately understand that there were things wrong with the status quo and that changes were being sought.

Of paramount concern was the recognition that many guards, uneducated as to the causes of the difficult if not incomprehensible behavior of their charges, would need to acquire new understandings if they were to carry out their responsibilities. How much understanding they could acquire was an unknown. How to go about educating them was the first task.

1
PRELIMINARY CONSIDERATIONS AND PLANNING
Some Historical Background.

Historical events, conditions and attitudes are always difficult to overcome. Somehow the negative is remembered longer and more vividly than the positive. I was dumfounded on one occasion to be asked if I would support a "Contract for Service" bill allowing a private entrepreneur to assume the financial cost of caring for a prisoner (submitting him to slave labor) in exchange for a prisoner's labor. This was a modification of the practice in the territorial prison at Seatco (Bucoda) whereby the State paid a contractor a fee per day to handle the prisoner while the contractor also profited from the fruits of the prisoner's labor. In fact, the original contractor built the territorial prison, suggesting how lucrative the contract business must have been.

Fortunately for the State of Washington, the contract business was outlawed before the Walla Walla institution got underway in 1887. Also abandoned was the use of ankle irons with connecting chains riveted in place and kept there throughout the entire period of incarceration. The irons permitted only the shortest of steps with each stride.

The Walla Walla institution, and later the Reformatory in Monroe, were historically not unlike many of the large correctional institutions of the time. Food was often bad because some merchants would unload on the institutions produce they could not sell on the open market. Cells were stacked on top of each other, giving the resident a feeling of being "put away" on the shelf to wait out the number of months or years until release.

Meals in Walla Walla and Monroe (opened in 1908) were almost always the same, devoid of taste and interest, and served in absolute quiet on long tables. The men were seated on only one side of the table; as they looked ahead, they saw only the backs of their fellow residents seated at the next table. In the early days of the institution and for far too long thereafter, there was nothing for the men to do. The rare

29

occasion when a visitor came to the institution created some break in the monotony for the resident although it was accompanied by a belittling experience: in the presence of a guest, the resident was required to stand at attention with his back to the wall.

The prison uniform, with its plain design and horizontal black and white stripes, left no question that the wearer was "one of them" and not "one of us," a differentiation that has persisted even with the addition of the chaplaincy and more democratic principles of government.

Conditions weren't sanitary and there was no running water in those early days. To put the finishing touches on the depreciation of the resident, he was given a spoon as his only utensil with which to eat from a tin plate. When returned to the barren cell, where not even writing materials were allowed, he was angry and agitated.

Is it any wonder that prison riots ensued?

These negative conditions were modified for the better from time to time. When I first visited Walla Walla and Monroe, there were small tables in the dining room and residents could visit with one another during meals. A turret affixed overhead on the dining room wall in Monroe that once held an armed guard during mealtime was no longer occupied. Cells in both institutions were cleaner and each had a toilet but the cell blocks still stacked human beings, one on top of another. Movies were shown at scheduled times, and men had assignments in prison jobs, Institution Industries, and the farms.

I have vivid recollections of the prison services for women who were housed in the buildings outside the walls at Walla Walla. The facilities were stark, with tiny cells coming off a long corridor. Some had curtains if the resident's family could afford to pay for the material. Many of the women did handwork — again, if families could provide them with the necessary materials and equipment. While the rooms might have been more pleasant than the men's cell blocks, the absence of activity (except for the exercise period) was startling. After the "routine" breakfast, the women were locked in their cells until lunch; and the monotony was repeated in the afternoon.

At the end of the long corridor were two "quiet" rooms, where women who were distressed and "out of control" were placed. They became "strip" cells, although the women were not deprived of their clothing as they entered. When once in the "quiet" rooms, their anxiety often led them to tearing their clothing to shreds. Isolation in dark confinement accentuated their problems. There were women attendants during most shifts, but at times a single male attendant was in charge. Among his duties was the distribution of sanitary napkins to the half-naked women in the seclusion area.

30

Some of the women residents felt free to discuss with me the treatment other female residents had experienced. They spoke of blackmail, "affairs," and pregnancies. Only one told me a personal experience. She remembered the date she had been struck by a male guard and knocked to the floor. She developed an "arthritic-like" pain in her jaw, which persisted for several years. But her ten years in prison had taught her to "take it" and she had kept quiet.

All of the women residents I interviewed spoke of the vulgar language and verbal abuse they experienced at the hands of the officers. Happily, the problems described were being corrected.

I am reminded of the first woman prisoner in the territorial prison who was housed in a cabin outside the walls of the institution. She was lucky!

Legislative Intent.

That the Washington State Legislature and many other state legislatures have long been seriously interested in treatment rather than punishment for offenders is demonstrated by the number of times the term "rehabilitation" appears in the various state codes.[4] Rehabilitation, of course, is always in the public's best interest. To rehabilitate means to advance the individual and help him or her in the effort to become a law abiding, productive citizen and taxpayer.

I have often wondered exactly what "rehabilitation" may have meant to the legislators of the past. Certainly they did not view rehabilitation as the extensive treatment process that many professional social scientists may see it to be. But, regardless of their understanding of the term, the emphasis on "rehabilitation" clearly implies a positive attitude toward the offender and defines the role of the institution serving him. Use of the word suggests a view of the offender as someone who can be helped, who should be helped and who, if helped, can become a better integrated member of society. The prison, with its resources, is the state's method of approaching the offender's problems.

With this view of legislative intent, it is difficult to accept the attitude of many correctional staffers in the past who referred to the residents in institutions as "animals" or "inmates" (with its negative connotation), or even as "hairy-assed sons of bitches" (a designation heard with some frequency in Washington State corrections in the 1950s and 1960s).

There is an old slogan which says, "You did your crime, now serve your time." The attitude conveyed in this phrase places emphasis on incarceration rather than on creating a therapeutic atmosphere in which may be found a new and improved relationship between the offender and those who are employed by the state to rehabilitate him. That therapeutic atmosphere, when properly implemented, is a learning environment in which the offender learns more productive ways of behaving as he associates with prison staff who are his teachers.

The laws creating correctional institutions assign to them responsibility to protect the public. This is both reasonable and logical. But to think of protecting the public only in terms of incarceration is not to protect the public. Under that narrow approach, the incarceration merely delays the threat to the public. A person should leave prison having a positive experience that has benefited him. That experience should have helped dissipate that individual's anger, made him feel more comfortable in relationships with others, and at the same time rendered him less of a threat to the world around him. Corrections officials who hold the attitude that their duty is to incarcerate without treating the offender are taking the easy way out. They are pleasing that segment of society that seeks immediate punishment and removal of the offender from society, but they aren't satisfying society's long-range need to change (treat) the offender's behavior so he may become an acceptable and productive member of society.

Garrett Heyns addressed this matter in 1967 in his paper, "The Treat 'em Rough Boys Are Here Again," published in *Federal Probation*, June 1967.

He wrote:

> Allied with the advocacy of the "Treat 'em Rough" program is the thought many have that rehabilitation of the delinquent and the prevention of delinquency are largely a matter of good policy, practice, speedy apprehension, followed, of course, by court action, hopefully severe. One hears this stress on speedy action by the police coming even from high places.
>
> There is no doubt as to the desirability of quick and efficient police action, that immediate apprehension is vital to stopping depredations of delinquent youth. However, those who talk about this matter speak as if it were the solution to the whole problem of delinquency. There seems to be no thought given here to the need of an attack upon the causes of delinquency. What makes delinquents of those whom we are seeking speedily to apprehend? Forgotten seems to be the fact that most of these delinquents and pre-delinquents ...have no code to which they can relate conduct save the pragmatic one — do that with which you can get by. Those who may have influenced them have never taught them any other code. Right and wrong are to them meaningless terms.

The administration of the Department of Institutions in Washington during the 1950s and 1960s felt a deep obligation to fulfill the expressed intent of the Legislature. Protection of the public, of course, was essential, but incarceration without rehabilitation was seen as irresponsible and illegal. The legislation called for both public protection *and* treatment. Speedy police and court action and incarceration were not enough. There was also a pressing need to understand the causes of the unacceptable behavior, to assist in the development of a code to which the incarcerated person might look for guidance, and to help the resident of the program learn to distinguish right from wrong and to do so with determination.

I don't want to oversimplify but it might make the issue more clear if I were to remind the reader of a common experience. Most families, I believe, will agree that their children accomplished the most in school years when they had pleasant and supporting relationships with their teachers. If there is a good feeling between an individual and that person's role models, then growth and emulation are possible. Obviously, the converse is also true. If there is discomfort between child and teacher, learning may come to a halt and angry feelings that are destructive to the child and those he knows may result.

If correctional staff are to accomplish their teaching mission, they must understand and accept those placed in their charge. At the very least, they need to approach them as human, regardless of how repugnant the offender's behavior may have been. What is there to lose by humane treatment? Only the sense of power and control over others, a countertherapeutic condition that has historically plagued the corrections field.

The 1960 phase of Washington's prison reform program looked to the creation of an atmosphere conducive to helping people change their bad behavior. It was recognized to be an uphill course.

Garrett Heyns, the seasoned teacher and prison administrator, often expressed doubt as to whether the creation of a more therapeutic atmosphere was possible. His doubt came from practical experiences in Michigan where he had been a prison warden. He felt that punitive attitudes were so deeply ingrained in prison staffs that changing them to rehabilitationists probably was impossible. But, difficult or impossible as it might be to help people change, he felt an effort had to be made. In what could well have been an unconscious prophecy, he mused:

> Getting people to change is like getting a new bill through the
> Legislature. You try, and try again, and each time a little bit more
> is learned and understood until, at last, changes are made and the
> bill gets through.

Heyns' position was even stronger in this regard in 1967 when he served as the Executive Director of the Joint Commission on Correctional Manpower and Training in Washington, D.C. Again, using his thesis, "The Treat 'em Rough Boys Are Here Again" and addressing primarily the problems of juveniles, he said:

> Another fact of which the "Treat 'em Rough" advocates should be reminded is that a program which emphasizes the punitive and one which stresses the corrective cannot go hand in hand. You cannot have a regimen which aims at severity and one that aims at understanding treatment in the same institution.

In the same paper, he commented:

> One sad point in regard to the contention of the the "Treat 'em Rough" advocates that progressive practices do not work is the fact that these practices have never been adequately implemented.

Neither Heyns nor I felt it would be possible to bring sufficient treatment staff into the institutions in Washington to make a substantial impact. After all, when he arrived on the scene even the state mental hospitals with their popular support and their bulging populations had only a handful of professional therapists. Further, to propose building additional institutions for the treatment of offenders, requiring even more staff and money, was in no way realistic. Obviously, existing structures had to be used and an effort had to be made to give the existing staff a more therapeutic orientation.

Some undertaking! The Washington State correctional facilities in the '50s and '60s were militaristic organizations.

The distance between the residents of the institutions and their "keepers" was confounding for the resident and inappropriate in any program financed by the taxpayers of the state. There was no way the correctional facilities could be viewed as carrying out the intent of the Legislature that convicted offenders be rehabilitated.

At that time, for instance, a resident of an institution who wanted an audience with a high-ranking prison official had to apply for an appointment and then wait an interminable time before he was given the opportunity to express a complaint about his care or to seek some assistance with a personal, social, or health problem.

There was no way in which such a situation could be interpreted as there being any real interest in the needs of the resident or his growth and development. His rehabilitation seemed not to be a consideration. But this was only the tip of the iceberg: communications barriers were so great we were doubtful the correctional services could come to be rehabilitative.

Staff Attitudes: A Basic Target.

Perhaps the greatest question in all of the efforts to change prisons revolved around the guards; those having the most contact with residents. Were they interested in changing their approach? Would they try to do so, and, would they change? How does one motivate for change? How does one bring about changes in attitudes and behavior?

Effective treatment in any situation depends upon positive contact and understanding between residents and staff. Establishing this is a big order in the traditional prison setting.

Many prison guards were children and grandchildren of prison guards. All too often, doing what was done before was more important to them than helping those who were "the kept." Others held guard jobs only while they were looking for something better or while they were in school preparing for their chosen careers. It would be difficult to find any serious dedication to the task of changing human behavior among this important staff. Sticking to traditional patterns is easier than making changes, particularly when there is no motivation for change and the rewards for making the changes are not readily obvious.

In 1966, a national survey revealed that there were no specific educational requirements for 41 percent of the correctional officer positions in state correctional facilities.[5] Only 47 percent of those positions carried salaries of $6,000 or more per year. Work in a correctional facility was looked on as a custodial job and nothing more. All the guards were expected to do was be present at the prison and keep residents from escaping.

It was no surprise, then, that many guards had little motivation to become a therapeutic agent in the Reform Movement.

The Washington correctional program was conducted in two, then four, institutions at the time of the Heyns-Conte Administrations. The older of these institutions were the state penitentiary at Walla Walla and the reformatory at Monroe. They were big, cumbersome institutions, steeped in tradition and hidden away in small communities. Both institutions were cut off from the mainstream of Washington life and located in communities that presented clearcut problems for the recruitment of new staff.

They were manned by many very dedicated individuals, some of whom were aware that the programs were counter-productive. Many knew that people left prison more angry and a greater risk to society than they were on admission.

For the most part, the staff felt they were doing a good job in guarding prisoners — and they were! But the institutions were staffed by a group who were essentially devoid of psychology-mindedness, who thought punishment was the answer to the crime problem and who seemed to ignore the fact that their efforts were counter-productive in spite of the warning of some administrative leaders who knew differently. The staff generally did not understand their clients, what those clients needed, and how their clients might be changed.

To summarize briefly the obstacles faced in trying to change attitudes and behaviors of prison guards in the '60s, one must note that:

a. Salaries of staff were not a motivational factor.

b. Learning from those who came before and from what had always been done was deeply ingrained.

c. Many guards did not plan to remain on their jobs very long — with the result that there wasn't much energy extended to "get with" something new.

d. The guards, generally, were uninformed about the people with whom they were working, and rehabilitation was a foreign idea. Further, the thought that treatment rather than punishment would better protect the society, was incomprehensible to most.

e. The contact with people who had committed crimes, many of them violent, must have evoked fear in the hearts of many of the "keepers."

f. Dealing with anger and violence of others on a daily basis has to make anyone fearful. That, in turn, could cause the "keepers" to act irrationally and with undue force. When people are scared they may have a tendency to lash out first to "beat the other to the punch."

Preparing For Change.

It was apparent from the outset in the search for new horizons in correctional programming that the Washington leadership needed to teach, espouse and practice certain basic information and ideas about human behavior and interpersonal relationships. As noted, this information was already known and was a part of all schools of learning, psychology, and sociology. Briefly stated, we felt a need:

a. To describe to staff why people behave as they do — even very troubled and angry people whose actions often defy interpretation.

b. To convey the message that understanding people is a first step in accepting them.

c. To help staff recognize that the more they understood about their charges, the more effective they could be as correctional personnel.

A second "bottom line" aspect of the preliminary planning was that of defining ways the message of humane treatment could be transmitted to staff and ways to engage them to actively participate in the entire Reform program. In organizations so large and widely scattered, it was abundantly clear that there would have to be many in-house training programs as well as ones that could provide a statewide coverage.

Washington's correctional system in the 1960s was plagued with antiquated job descriptions, a lack of interest in change, and a strong union prepared to resist new developments. There also was an almost total absence of a theoretical base concerning causes of criminal behavior — a lack that made progressive communication about clients and their problems impossible. The leadership in the Department of Institutions in the '50s and '60s never believed corrections personnel would be overjoyed when asked to develop new approaches to old problems. We did feel, however, that the opportunity to try methods that might prove more effective for the resident and more rewarding for the staff would hold an interest for some. We knew that at least these members of staff would be eager to develop better understanding of the people to be served.

We also knew that while changing the traditional methods and ideas would be difficult, changing traditional State government practices and procedures would be equally tough. And it was! Job descriptions held in high regard by unions were sometimes cast in stone and reflected traditional ideas about prisons and their personnel. They had been written in most instances by those who held the attitude that custody was the only reason for a prison. Such job descriptions encouraged employees who did not have the motivation to learn new ways of approaching people, or who did not want to change their ways. They rebelled at the idea of learning a new approach. Usually their job descriptions did not make mandatory the upgrading of skills or participation in formal educational activities. So, there was no on-the-job incentive to change. And, all too often, they were supported in their disinterest in change by their union leadership which feared that the "liberals" in charge were going to eliminate jobs. After all, if the program was successful, populations might be reduced and it might not be necessary to have so many people employed in these institutions.

But the job descriptions weren't the only stumbling block. Very few of the correctional staff had had any preparatory work, not even an orientation other than what they had acquired in the institution, i.e., an orientation to the traditional. These were days before community colleges offered a curriculum in corrections.

In addition, courses offered at the universities were presented at a level requiring considerably more academic background than most correctional officers had. Sometimes these programs were not particularly practical in their orientation, and they weren't designed with training needs of the correctional officers in mind. This became very evident in the '60s when most of the people coming out of the country's formal training programs in each of the disciplines required by state services were notably more capable in theory than they were in practice.

2
A BASIC SCIENCE FOR CORRECTIONS

We have long postulated and clearly stated that it is an absolute necessity to have a theoretical concept as to why criminal behavior has evolved before one can be an effective participant in any treatment endeavor. To proceed without an idea as to how the behavior has come to be is as foolhardy as it would be for an electrician to attempt to repair a television set with no knowledge of the circuitry. There are a number of theories on the development of criminal behavior; thus, regardless of personal endowment or academic background, one can find a theory that is understandable and within which one will be able to work.

In parallel with this fundamental requirement is the necessity that each institution have its own basic concepts of human behavior and treatment which can be endorsed by most staff. Such a position helps define the objectives and goals of the program. While one would not expect all staff to hold the same theoretical position on the development of criminal behavior, any approach which is not in conflict with that of the parent institution greatly enhances the communication between staff and the effectiveness of the individual staff member. Understandings of this sort are essential to treatment of the offender, an activity in which every staff person could and would, hopefully, play a key role.

In an effort to instill a theoretical concept I have, in many programs both in Washington and elsewhere, described a simple chain reaction. It is a concept that has appeal both at the college and high school levels and has seemed to catch on with any number of institution staff — provided, of course, there is a receptive attitude toward learning new concepts. It might best be described as a psychological approach with emphasis on stimulus-response phenomenon.

The presentation of this concept, made repeatedly formally and informally to Washington's corrections staff in the '60s, incorporated terms and phenomena that are readily understood. In essence, this concept is as follows:

1) Everyone is subjected periodically to a clash between himself and others, between his ideals and those of the rest of the world, and between his ambitions and abilities to accomplish those ambitions.

2) Obviously, when the individual turns out to be the winner in a conflict there is no reason for concern. The person is happy and has no reason to act out adversely. But if, in fact, the desires of the individual are thwarted in the conflict, (such as in the case of an individual who has never gained recognition or approval), that person experiences the next step in the chain reaction: a sense of frustration.

3) Frustration implies the inability to acquire what one wants or needs. And, frustration is never experienced without a degree of anger.

4) Ill-controlled feelings of anger are not well tolerated in any culture. In fact, there are those who are officially appointed to intervene and respond to the untoward effects of anger that has gotten out of hand. This is a fundamental societal expectation.

5) But anger is not necessarily the end of the chain reaction. When anger is intense and not appropriately discharged, it becomes associated with fear (anxiety). This inevitable psychological reaction seems to be the result of a recognition, often denied or repressed, that living with anger leads to more conflict with people and the threat they will retaliate. Thus, the individual's problem is confounded. He has not only his hostility with which to deal but his anxiety to handle as well. All too often, the handling of this complex matter results in "acting out" which, if antisocial in character, may call again for legal intervention, more conflict, etc.

6) One working in the correctional system needs to understand that the residents in his care are both angry and frightened, and that the behavior which brought an individual to the correctional facility was a defense against the painful distress occasioned by this untenable combination of psychological experiences.

For individuals who ultimately become residents of prisons, the behaviors which defend against anxiety have been universally undesirable.

They are characterized by a sense of disinterest and selfishness, and a demand that "I want what I want, when I want it," and if anxiety is sufficiently intense, "I will do whatever it takes to get what I want."

Individuals so plagued live a life that is self-centered and non-caring. They acquire a basic dysfunctional characterological position; their total being becomes absorbed in acquiring what they want without regard for the feeling of others; they may commit violence against others; and they may disregard social custom and legal constraints as they do what they want to do without consideration of possible consequences.

These individuals often irritate and exasperate others, prison guards included, because their behavior clearly disguises the fact of their profound fright. The chain reaction explanation of criminal behavior is straightforward and easily understandable.

It may be enough to enable persons working in corrections to come to understand the strange and recalcitrant behavior of their clients.

If criminal behavior is to be changed and the discordant way of life discontinued, one must respond to the factors that brought about the acting-out in the first place. A first step in the approach to the corrections client is the development of an understanding of those causal factors.

The school of thinking in psychology that has been described here is basically a psychoanalytical position. A more rigid adherence to deeper psychological concepts would not find fault with the chain reaction approach we have found to be effective in teaching. The analysts would, however, be more concerned with deeper intra-psychic conflicts and the unconscious.

While some of our staff were intent in their study, usually only those who were pursuing graduate degrees wanted to take the time to learn the new vocabulary that was often necessary to understand other psychological or psychobiological concepts.

(I think it also worthy of note that even twenty years ago the issue of genetics and organicity in the development of human behavior was not given much credence, some studies of the Department of Institutions to the contrary notwithstanding.)[6]

In our campaign to understand criminal behavior, we placed heavy emphasis on the teaching of the sociologist. Some found that approach more palatable than a strictly psychological approach.

Sociologists have always been interested in group and environmental influences on individual behavior. The groups that attract the greatest attention are the disadvantaged who tend to congregate in the city centers or ghettos. It is well known that idleness occupies an unreasonable portion of the time of all age groups who live in the ghetto. The lack of interesting activity with a constructive slant is clearly apparent in such areas. In addition, those who are caught up in such conditions often feel trapped and lose their motivation for trying to move themselves ahead.

It is a truism that prisons incarcerate a large number of individuals who have come from desperately deprived backgrounds. They often have a history of dropping out of school, of having started their criminal careers with juvenile crimes that either escaped the attention of the courts or have been dealt with inadequately, and of having a host of social problems.

The sociologist will always remind one that the impact on learning in such a negative environment is exceedingly powerful and, unfortunately, the pace setters tend to perpetuate the distress by virtue of the unhealthy example they show to younger generations.

William T. Adams, sociologist in residence in the Department of Institutions from 1965 to 1972, and an outstanding teacher in the Reform Movement, wrote extensively on the subject of criminal delinquency. Much of his writing was published by the Department of Institutions.

Adams notes:

> ...The dynamics of deviant behavior are perhaps best explained through a synthesis of the individual in his social setting and the details of his life experience. The child is born into a social system, and he experiences an ongoing process of solving problems. Ideally, he learns roles which expedite his movement in the cultural surroundings. He internalizes ways of doing things that are sanctioned by his fellow members, and he adapts inner control devices which regulate his behavior in the social surroundings. He incorporates the general value system of the culture, but usually continually reexamines it. The society installs social controls which assist in insuring his harmonious adjustment. These statements about the normal socialization process are generally accepted. If the process works with individuals, the chances of deviancy are less likely than if it breaks down at various points...

> Some popular and long-standing notions about causation seek to expose society as the chief villain in the drama of crime and delinquency. Obviously, there is some truth to this point. Two cautions are needed: individuals are involved, and American society is not monolithic. Contradictions are plentiful in society's complex of values, norms, demands, and expectations. Social crises, such as the prohibition that some racial and ethnic groups cannot share the full meaning of society, are real.

Deprivation of success, authority, and the future appears in the lives of many persons throughout the land: in large urban settings with mobile minority groups, in suburban neighborhoods in a visibly affluent society, in small towns where detection is easy and resources are limited, in rural areas and among migrant farm laborers. Case histories in any correctional agency illustrate the point readily...[7]

One could not adequately cover the issue of causation in criminal behavior without a mention of the theological approach. While a religious philosophy could scarcely be viewed as a school of thinking, it is clear that many individuals who enter prisons are without a philosophical view of themselves, their place in the world, or their future. The Department recognized the need to approach this condition in its continuing struggle to add chaplains to the staff in the correctional facilities. The spiritual enlightenment the chaplains brought, together with their counseling skills, pleased many who looked on the teachings of Jesus Christ as guidelines for rehabilitation of the offender.

These summary comments on theories of behavior have described a number of points of view concerning the development of criminal behavior. The hope of the administration in the 1950s and 1960s was that every staff person would hear these concepts and develop some ideas for himself as to why his charges had behaved as they had. With a philosophy of his own, the staff person would be better equipped to provide rehabilitative services.

The purist among the staff was pleased with these concepts because he could identify with the psychologist, the sociologist, and other theorists. The eclectic was equally pleased. He could adopt the best of all possible worlds. These materials were presented repeatedly in various forums from institutional class-rooms to seminars in the ghetto. The opportunities to learn from formal instruction and from observations on the street were legion.

3
THE HEYNS ERA

It would be difficult to set a date establishing the actual time the modern-day Reform Movement became a reality in the State of Washington. Certainly it was clearly launched by the mid 1950s. Several significant developments, together with his own philosophical view, caused Robert A. Freeman, Assistant Superintendent and Director of Education at the Washington State Penitentiary to write in *Perspective*, a Department publication, in June, 1957 as follows:

> The problem of what to do with law breakers has plagued mankind for thousands of years. Today, overwhelming evidence shows the futility of past punitive measures, while all evidence grows to support the theory that by careful diagnosis and treatment of criminals, crime can be abated.[8]

> Washington is accenting this new philosophy at the 70-year-old State Penitentiary at Walla Walla. Housing completed in 1887 and obsolete workshops are being razed to make way for modern new ones. In order to give prisoners intelligent guidance and encourage them to reform, the prison must have facilities specifically adapted to develop that concept. p.7

Mr. Freeman reported on the new construction, including the minimum security building, where each person could live under less restraint and supervision. He noted that in minimum security:

> Each man has his own neatly appointed room; after working hours he comes and goes much as he pleases inside stipulated boundaries. Diminishing parole violations by these men prove the money for the construction was well spent. p.7

After noting that morale improved with the opening of a new mess hall, Mr. Freeman comments on the recently acquired permanent headquarters for the reception-guidance unit. He says:

> The unit is staffed with a sociologist in charge, a clinical psychologist and a vocational counselor ...reports are...compiled from responses sent to the family and friends, prior employers and schools, law enforcement and other public agencies and a summary of the history is prepared for the man's prison file to be used by the parole board and the prison staff.

It would appear that Freeman and his colleagues in Walla Walla were enthusiastic in their acceptance of the better facilities and the opportunity for a more humane treatment approach to their charges.

Writing in *Perspective* in August 1957, Tye Hagman (administrative assistant at the Reformatory and later newspaperman in northern Washington) commented on new developments at the State Reformatory. He said, in part:

> No (resident) can be expected to assume full responsibility of citizenship in a free community unless he is given as much responsibility as he can assume while serving his time...(Thus) some institutional changes include the privilege of leaving the dining room without a guard escort, cancellation of the requirement that (residents) stand up to the bars of their cells for the count, and the establishment of an honor block where 80 men live in unlocked cells and come and go within much of the institution at their own pleasure...

> On the extra-curricular side, a well-rounded athletic program is handled by an athletic supervisor, including both intramural and varsity football (and) basketball. Several hundred (residents) belong to organizations such as Alcoholics Anonymous, Toastmasters, Explorers Club, Bible Study, Fellowship, and both regular and special religious services, etc. p.6

Of particular significance in view of later developments was an Advisory Council to which Mr. Hagman referred as follows:

> The Inmate Advisory Council is expected to assist in the advancement of the program. An 11-man body, elected quarterly by the inmates, the IAC is a liaison between "inmates" and administration. Members meet weekly to consider...requests, suggestions and 'beefs,' of which those considered worthwhile are submitted to the superintendent. p.6

Publications of the Department of Institutions in the same period as the Freeman and Hagman writings emphasized the legislative hopes. Bills were introduced calling for more staff to speed the rate of resident rehabilitation, a reception and diagnostic center for juveniles, another bill calling for the replacement of "vintage" structures at Walla Walla, and even an emergency 200-kilowatt power plant for one of the correctional facilities was requested!

Among the notable accomplishments of the program in 1957 was the launching of an honor system for residents of the facility at Monroe. One of the farms was renamed "Honor Farm" and with its new name came a new administrative structure. The objective of the program was to delegate ever-increasing responsibilities to the resident assigned to live and work there, thus providing a smoother transition from prison to parole status.

In addition, in June 1957, twenty-nine men graduated from high school at ceremonies in the Walla Walla prison and twenty-one additional diplomas were awarded for the completion of "grammar school."

And Fort Warden, a new juvenile institution, came on line as a member of the institution family.

These forward-looking changes in the correctional system were enhanced by the headline announcement in August 1957, "Noted Penologist Appointed Director of Institutions." The announcement, as recorded in *Perspective*, advised that Dr. Garrett Heyns, "a veteran Michigan penologist," had been appointed by Governor Albert D. Rosellini to become the director of the Department of Institutions. It added that Dr. Heyns had had twenty years of experience with the Michigan system and that he was the third professional with graduate training to hold that position. The new Director was highly respected, and the stage was set for new and creative developments.[9]

Garrett Heyns was 66 years of age when he came to the State of Washington. He had had a broad experience in state governmental operations. He knew the frustrations of dealing with legislatures who had first to be educated on needs and then convinced to appropriate monies to meet those needs. He was also well acquainted with political influence in public programs: Michigan was rather sophisticated as regards political maneuverings while Washington politics at the time were quite naive. In Michigan, Heyns had felt pressure from elected officials on the one hand and from staff and organized labor on the other.

For Heyns, coming to Washington was a carefully considered matter. He was coming at an age when many would think of retirement. He had already had two careers: an academic one where he had taught at both the preparatory and university level, and the correctional career in which he had been a warden. Wasn't that enough? Would he not be looked on as already having retired and coming to enjoy the beauties of the Northwest?

Heyns and his family were easily able to answer these questions. He would not come to retire or to sightsee. He was vigorous and spirited. He would come because of the challenge and because the

Directorship of the Department of Institutions offered him the opportunity to put ideas, philosophies and techniques into effect. This was something he had always wanted to do but had never quite had the free hand with which to do it.

As he considered the position in Washington, he felt it would not have serious political complications for him because he was so experienced in dealing with such issues. On the other hand, the extent of unionization within Washington State government was a shock. (Little was he to know that state government in Washington stood on the verge of an era that would see far greater union influence.)

Garrett Heyns had serious questions about the unionization of The People's services. He was always the first to define and support the rights of employees in any discussion. He felt union members deserved protection from abuse in their employment and they should be helped in every way possible to enjoy personal and employment advancement. But unions carry within them the possibility of strikes. How could one allow even a moment to pass when those in his care might be without the services they were guaranteed by law to receive? Surely there must be a better way to protect the employees of state government than unionization.

Although the matter of unionization was not a question open for debate, the topic was one of continuing discussion and Heyns repeatedly reevaluated his position as he proceeded with his administrative duties.

Heyns did have another solution — one that was at the heart of his character and administrative style. He felt that as the director of a program, he was a director of all those who worked in that program. The interests of each employee were his to understand and protect. And he did, with great fairness and objectivity.

This philosophy had been thoroughly defined in his discussions with Governor Albert D. Rosellini about becoming Director of Institutions in Washington and was manifest much later in such developments as arranging time for employees to advance their educational goals, and in making decisions that were clearly in the favor of the employees, the ambitions of the various administrators notwithstanding.

Heyns sincerely believed, and often demonstrated, that when he and an unhappy employee were left to their own resources, and were allowed to express their concerns and goals freely, the interests of the employee were better addressed.

Politics and unionization entered into his negotiations with the Governor. Both Rosellini and the would-be Director knew there was little they could do about union influence. But politicians were another matter. Governor Rosellini promised Heyns there would be no political influence from his office, and he said he would do all he could to protect Heyns from political interferences from elsewhere. When the guarantee came in writing, Heyns was prepared to assume his new job in Institutions.

Given a free hand and strong gubernatorial support and protection, Heyns introduced and demanded a high degree of professionalism. He felt the State — that is, *all* the people — deserved quality service, and he saw it as the responsibility of state government operations to provide that "best" quality. Clearly, he viewed the Department of Institutions as a service organization that needed to operate with high academic standards. This view led to the appointment of professional leadership in all the disciplines at both the central office level and in the field.

The new Director held yet another ambition. He looked forward to a day when existing institutions could be organized into smaller units and newer institutions be tailored to meet the needs of specific groups.[10] He felt that such institutions would maximize treatment opportunity and success. In addition, he hoped that institutions of the future would be supervised by a "Board of Regents." Using that designation would, he thought, let it be known that the programs were always in pursuit of an academic orientation, and that they held high the hope for quality treatment programs. Such a development would also give public institutions the kind of protection from political manipulation enjoyed by institutions of higher learning.

He often mentioned that the qualifications for his position were spelled out in the law, with primary emphasis on the academic background required for the appointment. He was the first to suggest training requirements be written into job descriptions for any new position created in the Department of Institutions.

Heyns deplored the rumbles heard nationally (at that time) calling for a consolidation of state programs under an umbrella agency. He spoke strongly against such developments to both governors with whom he worked in Washington, believing that consolidation would create new problems and increase costs rather than solve difficulties less expensively, as advocates often said. The new Director arrived with a spirit of excitement and enthusiasm, and he was quickly accepted across the state. His was quality leadership. He could address a legislative committee and point out the shortcomings of their previous actions while at the same time making his comments palatable.[11]

◊◊◊◊◊

The first months of the Heyns administration were filled with getting acquainted and learning the ropes. The Department at that time had 23 separate institutions in a variety of areas: mental health, retardation, juvenile and adult corrections, parole services, schools for the deaf and blind, and residential services for veterans. Just learning where these programs were located and what personnel was involved in them was a monumental task. Even so, Heyns busied himself with projects started before his arrival, with developing new ones and with planning. The opportunity to build something new and better was waiting to be exploited.

◊◊◊◊◊

A cursory review of *Perspective* reveals both the forward movement of the organization and Heyns' instantaneous influence. Some headlines and excerpts follow:

November 1957 *Groundwork is Started For Implementing Department's Division on Alcoholism.*
> The goals of this program are: treatment, research and education.

December 1957 *Department Will Publish First Annual Report on Adult Corrections.*
> About 1500 copies are expected to be printed and this edition will mark the first time that any division within the Department has published a report for public distribution. The issue will report on the State Bureau of Criminal Identification, program progress at the penitentiary, the reformatory, and the two honor camps, and tables and diagrams covering prisoner characteristics, institutional population and parole statistics.

January 1958 *Imprisoned Men and Women Observe Christmas Reverence.* This will be the first midnight Christmas Mass ever held in the maximum security building of the Washington State Penitentiary.

January 1958 *Honor Camp Chapel Opens on Christmas.* Inmates of the Larch Mountain Honor Camp had their first religious service in their new interdenominational chapel at 10 a.m. Christmas morning. This chapel has been nearly 2 years in construction and has been constructed mainly by volunteer inmate labor. The bricks in the construction came from both the Washington State Penitentiary and the Washington State Reformatory, from walls and buildings that had been torn down. The glass, woodwork, mortar and cement, as well as other materials which were necessary to purchase have been financed by contributions from the Vancouver Rotary Club, the Vancouver Council of Churches, the Christian Science Committee for Institutional Work, and other interested people.

April 1959 *Penitentiary Adds Vocational School.*
Quoting Robert A. Freeman, "The new vocational building has been completed for the educational program of the state penitentiary...The program will specialize in auto mechanics, machine shop, and office machine repairs."

July-August 1959 *Penitentiary Building Program Progresses.*
A section of the Washington State Penitentiary hospital and an older cell block will be razed soon in preparation for one of the biggest building programs in the history of the institution. Architects have nearly completed plans for a new hospital wing and are working on plans for replacing cell blocks 4 & 5.

October 1959 *Doctor Heyns Wins Secretarial Post at Annual American Correctional Administrators' Association.*
He will attend the 89th Annual Congress in Florida...Lawrence Delmore, Supervisor of the Division of Adult Corrections, also will attend that meeting.

Summer 1959 *Two New Honor Camps to be Built.*
Department of Natural Resources construction program includes $435,500 for the construction of two new adult honor camps and the expansion of another during the biennium, according to Land Commissioner Bert Cole. These call for the construction of a camp near Loomis, in Okanogan County, and another in the Washougal area of Skamania County. Expansion of the Larch Mountain Camp to house 100 inmates is currently under way.

March 1960 *Pre-Released Programs Reorient Inmates to Outside.*
There are 175 persons returned to Washington State institutions from parole during the 1959 fiscal year, while 852 inmates won parole. Pre-release programming at Washington State Penitentiary and the Washington State Reformatory are designed to assist in the high parole rate program of the State Board of Prison Terms and Parole. Inmates nearing expiration of their sentences may go to pre-release programs for 30 days prior to release, according to the plans.

August 1960 New field house at Monroe will result in major expansion of reformatory's recreation program.

The Heyns Program and Approach.

Assuming the responsibility for twenty-three separate institutions and a host of community programs was thought provoking and time consuming. But Garrett Heyns loved it! And, in one way or another, he devoted his every waking moment to it. He traveled across the state and attended meetings of every organization in which it appeared there might be an interest in "The People's Programs." In addition, he was a nationally known and respected authority in the field of corrections and his talents were demanded by a broad range of organizations and committees.

But all was not well. As the months and years went by, it became clear that there were problems inherent in the Department that needed to be solved even as new programs of better quality were being implemented.

Some of the problems were a nearly total surprise. Bookkeeping procedures, accounting practices and guidelines for accountability were grossly inadequate, and personnel practices, looked on with favor by many old-timers in state government, were simply inadequate to support the new and improved programs Heyns envisioned.

In addition, while he discovered many time-honored and very devoted staff in the Department, the experience of many was limited to their current jobs and they were not attuned to another way of doing things. As expected, Heyns met resistance when he suggested change. "We have always done it this way," he was told. His reply: "I know."

Although greatly diversified in his obligations to the broad range of the Department's responsibility, he always found time to approach the problems in corrections. As competent individuals were recruited for the other divisions in the Department, he had more and more time to study problems in the correctional system and to extend his influence in planning there.

With his background as an educator and his observations that previous efforts in corrections were ineffective, he had come to see treatment for offenders in correctional institutions as the only hope for the future. I am sure he would have heartily endorsed the writings of Freeman and Hagman quoted earlier. Heyns' main concern was: how does one get the point across?

Wherever he spoke or participated in discussions he expressed the need for change and emphasized that change in people could be expected only with humanitarian treatment. How many times he must have said, "Treatment of the man in prison must be different than the negative 'handling' he has known before."

Translated to the language of my field, he was noting again and again that the best learning takes place in an atmosphere of respect and understanding.

Heyns insisted that the "rehabilitation" called for in the statutes required the resolution of negative feelings toward offenders and a change in attitude toward them. He saw this as the key to helping offenders develop new and more productive patterns of behavior.

From his devotion, focus and energy, there emerged a methodical approach to the needs of the Department of Institutions and to corrections in Washington. Although it was never defined as a plan of action, one can, in retrospect, define the general principles and interests pursued as the Heyns program emerged. I outline them here and will elaborate on the significance of each step.

I.   Attention to business practices. Heyns felt that without a strong business and accounting service and progressive personnel practices, it would not be possible to better organize existing programs and to recruit greatly needed staff.

II.   Recruitment. Although Heyns found much competence in the Washington correctional system, there was a need for more help from a variety of schools of thought and from various disciplines.

III.   Professional growth and development. Without the opportunity for growth and development of staff, any significant program developments would be short-lived.

IV.   Creation of an environment conducive to the stimulation of the interest, enthusiasm, and desire for change so necessary and usually so lacking among residents of correctional programs and their staffs.

Early in his Washington experience, Heyns relied heavily upon an executive manager, Mr. Sidney Coleman, to assume major responsibilities for business matters in the Department, an endeavor that could not have been more appropriate at the time. There was an urgent need to upgrade business practices to enable the Director to concentrate on policy and make deliberate decisions about new programming. Further, some of the old procedures, such as keeping cash in a shoe box under the counter in one of the institutions, had to stop.

Heyns also came to know and appreciate the talents of Leonard Nord, whom he quickly appointed Director of Personnel for the Department. Nord had a wide variety of personnel experience in state government. His competence was recognized again later when he became Director of the State Department of Personnel, a position he was to hold for many years.

Nord had an unusual talent: he viewed his work as that of assisting program people in accomplishing that which they determined would be sound program development. He completely endorsed the Heyns position that "Nothing here is sacred. Everything can be changed!"

With Sidney Coleman in charge of business operations and Leonard Nord in Personnel, Heyns had the first of a long series of sound administrators to assist him. These two men were strongly supported in their undertakings.

Recruitment, an ongoing process in every governmental agency, was of great concern to Garrett Heyns.

Getting new people who would bring new ideas into corrections, and individuals who could support and enhance the creativity of existing staff, was his goal. Heyns expected those involved in recruitment to approach possible recruits with enthusiasm and with honesty. The potential for progressive program developments existed in Washington; but Washington was not there yet! "Come help with a new experiment," and "Help us overcome the tragedy of the past century," were his words of invitation. Leonard Nord and several of the Department's superintendents proved to be excellent recruiters. They had caught the spirit and they could pass it along! But, what were people being recruited into? How might they come to see where Washington State corrections was going?

In the unfolding of the Heyns era, certain logical developments answered some of the questions. Specifically, there was the formal identification of a philosophy of administration conducive to professional growth and development, and strong endorsement of staff involvement in professional organizations and committees.

The Heyns administrative experience had clearly illustrated that no one administrator or person in a leadership role could ever "do it alone." Further, when changes were needed, collective thinking and trust were essential. Ideas had to be stimulated, cultivated and encouraged, and every person involved had to be encouraged to express himself freely, without reservation. Only with the participation of all staff could the rehabilitative effort be fully realized.

Heyns expressed this view freely; staff and potential recruits were encouraged to become involved in the program. It was a position not easily understood by those steeped in the restraints of governmental employment; but, it was sweet music in what was otherwise a rather sterile and severely restricted program.

Heyns felt the best way to illustrate the seriousness of his commitment was to make certain that leaders of various programs

54

participated heavily in their own professional organizations. His position was well accepted by Governor Rosellini, and dollars flowed from state coffers to pay for travel to local and national professional meetings and conferences. "There is no better way for staff to learn what their compatriots are doing than go off some place and sit with them for a few days," Heyns often said.

Within a few years, staff in corrections were representing the State of Washington and benefiting from extensive collaboration with their professional colleagues around the country.

Involvement by department officials in more than fifty professional and governmental committees, task forces, and organizations left no doubt about the dedication to change of the leadership in the Department of Institutions.[12]

Uppermost in the thinking of Director Heyns was his ambition to see an end to the dehumanizing management of residents of correctional facilities and the creation of an environment conducive to the development of motivation for change. He knew this was a monumental task, given the reality that the so-called "treatment" of offenders up to that time had given first consideration to control and not to the encouragement of self improvement.

I think it quite certain that he never missed an opportunity to use a problem, a program, or a new development to comment on this goal. When he discussed Institution Industries he emphasized the value of work to the mental health of the individual. When, with the aid of the institutional Industries Commission, he organized the Committee of One Hundred Industrialists, he noted the group would advise the department on the work being done; but he suggested the people-to-people contact with active business persons would give residents a sense of worthwhileness. The residents would come to believe they were worthwhile individuals if people from the community came to Monroe to talk to them.

He again asserted his position concerning humane management of institutional residents when he conferred with the Washington Citizens' Council in the Spring of 1960. He noted that the record of the Larch Mountain Honor Camp was a good one. (Reported in *Perspective*, February 1960.) He quoted the record, indicating that during 1959, some 31,000 snags averaging 50 inches in diameter were felled by correctional resident crews. In addition, 415 acres had been prepared, 302 acres seeded, and 333,000 seedlings had been planted. But, he went on, as exciting as this was, there was no way to compare it to gains in human value received by those who participated. They were troubled men who had worked for the opportunity to live a more normal life in camp rather than in a cell. They had been trusted with the camp assignment and they had seen — maybe for the first time — some tangible result of their own efforts and investment. This, he told the Commission, was the true value of the Honor Camp System.

The Director was always on the lookout for teaching resources, formal or informal, and he saw in the Western Interstate Commission for Higher Education a much needed resource. Heyns became a member of the WICHE board of directors shortly after coming to Washington.

In *Perspective*, November 1960, an early-day participant of the WICHE program reported:

> WICHE was begun in 1953. This organization encompasses the 13 western states, and it was formed for the purpose of pooling western states resources so that a higher caliber of education and training could be provided for persons from these states in certain selected fields. p.4

The headquarters of the undertaking were at the University of Colorado in Boulder, and a broad range of institutions and universities were utilized as sites for the many training endeavors.

Heyns was always deeply involved in community undertakings, such as bond issues, libraries, the development of The Evergreen State College, and he functioned well at both the legislative and the local levels in furthering such projects.

He admonished staff to open the doors of the institution to the community. He viewed it as an exercise in self review when staff explained themselves to the community, and the open door policy was obviously beneficial in the public relations efforts. In *Perspective*, February, 1960, he told institution staff:

> It would be very good policy for institution administration to invite visitors from all over the state, but particularly from the local community, to go through the institution and learn of its programs. Obviously, groups such as service clubs, church organizations and the like, should be invited, but so should unattached citizens. Time has long since passed when institutions have any need for keeping things away from the public. So let's invite the public in to see for itself. What we have is worth showing. p.2

The Washington Corrections Center for Men

Perhaps the crowning event of Heyns' tenure with the Department of Institutions was his direction and supervision of the building of the Washington Corrections Center in Shelton. It had been a lifelong dream of his to build a correctional facility that would replace the aura of a prison with both the image and meaning of a college campus. It would be geared to the support of the human character of those who came there even though that quality was sometimes very difficult to find in them. The new institution would concentrate on diagnosis and treatability. In a pamphlet prepared by the public relations office of the Department, the Washington Corrections Center is described thusly:

> One of the newest, most modern and most unusual adult institutions in the world was placed in operation late in 1964 on 400 acres of a former homestead ranch five miles northwest of Shelton, Washington. The Washington Corrections Center is actually two institutions in one…a maximum security reception-diagnostic center, and a medium custody residential training center…

> The residential program at the Washington Corrections Center is designed to offer the finest possible institutional services for young first offenders…those most likely to make successful new lives for themselves, given proper guidance, training and education…

> The residential training unit, with a present capacity of 480, must, under existing law, serve as a secure place of custody for its residents, but it was designed to be far more than a mere barred warehouse for society's rejects. Simply stated, its primary purpose is to rehabilitate young first offenders and return them to society as good citizens before they become professional criminals.

> Its functional purpose is evident in its appearance, which has been described as resembling a modern college campus rather than a prison…

> So it is that one of the most impressive buildings on the 100-acre "campus" is Garrett Heyns High School, which includes 14 well-equipped classrooms where teachers of the Shelton School District conduct a fully accredited high school curriculum.

> The carefully planned lack of prison atmosphere is reflected in an absence of stereotyped prison attitudes. Although the young men assigned to the training unit at Washington Corrections Center have, for the time being, lost their liberty, they have been allowed to retain their self respect and human dignity.

> And human dignity needs space to breathe.

The Heyns Legacy

Garrett Heyns had fulfilled his dream and kept his promise: He had built a correctional institution that could demonstrate the value of humane treatment.

By 1966, Garrett Heyns had many fine accomplishments to look back on. He had developed a favorable public attitude towards "The People's Institutions" and had successfully stimulated interest on many fronts in pursuing something new and more effective in correctional programming. He had seen the transformation of a public program into one that was highly professional and on the move. There were four honor camps, a parole service more closely related to the correctional program, and a parole board that maximized the opportunity to release people from prison when the time was right for them to be released. He was an active supporter of job therapy, a special program created to assist releasees in finding jobs.

And the Department of Institutions was responsible for the State's jail inspection program. (Heyns had found another arena in which to spread the word about humane treatment and rehabilitation.)

Although Heyns entertained no thought that the Washington task was completed, he recognized clearly that Reform was in motion. He had defined what his contributions would be and he had carried out his commitment. He had made his point.

There was yet another career for Heyns in retirement. He was asked to be a member of the National Board of the Joint Commission on Correctional Manpower and Training. So he left the Directorship of the Department in September 1966 to seek new areas to explore in Washington D.C. He had served in Washington State under two governors, and both were generous in their commendation for a job well done.

4
SOME CONCURRENT DEVELOPMENTS

Although I am unaware of other prison reform movements at that time incorporating such a broad base of activity as that of the Washington effort, there were a number of developments, both nationally and locally, which came to have far-reaching effects on the Washington State program.

The 1960s were years dedicated to renewed demands for civil rights. They were years of venting hostilities, demonstrations about many issues in many places, and times when there were high hopes for righting wrongs. While many of the sought after changes were very important and long overdue, it was necessary, I felt, that each wrong be approached on the basis of sound reasoning and changes made in a deliberate and well thought out manner.

That period in our history will be remembered as the time of the emergence of the Black Power Movement. Black studies were introduced into many college and high school curricula. Black groups were organized and hostilities which had been repressed for 200 years were brought out into the open and frankly discussed.

With the leadership of Martin Luther King, Jr., attention to the black causes was given high priority, a position which was greatly intensified with the loss of the martyred black leader.

It was understandable that prisons became a focus of concern for black groups and others who were upset over the discrimination and abuse to which black residents were subjected. One did not have to look far to find evidences: prison populations have long had a disproportionate number of blacks in their general populations and on death rows suggesting the attitude of the general public as well as the prejudice of the courts in regard to black offenders.

The Black Power Movement encouraged blacks to hold their heads high, to view their black heritage with pride and to be assertive in the face of opposition. The spirit of the movement created enthusiasm for the mission. However, with negative feelings running so high and the sense of urgency among the black activists in the prison system so very great, I feared that the speedy and hard hitting style of some of the black organizations would stimulate resistance in ways which would inhibit progress.

Many thought that the passage of the Civil Rights Act in 1964 would give blacks reassurance that their condition was understood and that things would change, but this was not to be. Resistance to the civil rights measure was strong and progress of the black caucus was slow with the result that there emerged a black militancy of considerable proportions. Many blacks and their several organizations were ready to openly fight prejudice and to insist on equal treatment as provided in the Constitution but denied them from the beginning of the Republic. A trend toward the conservative created opposition to them. The battle lines were drawn.

The Black Panthers was a national organization ready to be counted. And, they were very knowledgeable about the treatment blacks had received in the nation's courts and prisons. They were resolved to carry on the necessary crusade to change bad conditions wherever they saw them.

My orientation to the Black Panthers began with a call from the Governor's office indicating that a representative from the Black Panthers wanted to see me. We met in what proved to be a very interesting session. The representative began with a clearly-stated position as to what some black organizations of the time were going to do: they would take over the prisons in the United States!

My visitor gave me a rather detailed statement concerning the abuse of blacks and other minorities in prisons. He was angry about these matters and was, at times, a bit threatening, but what he told me was true and I knew it. Before our conversation ended he understood that I, too, knew the facts about prisons and minorities.

When I inquired about the plans of the black organizations to which he had referred, he advised that the organizational structure was already in place and they knew how to proceed. They were dedicated to the concept that wrongs of the past had to be corrected. We shared some common concerns and hopes, and his hostile approach abated. When I declared my hope that we could see orderly change, he became upset. When I told him the veto power of the superintendents was likely to mean a slower progression of events than he would like, he responded loudly, "Fuck your veto power."

A few days after my encounter with the Black Panther, I received a letter from Jane Fonda.

Ms. Fonda's letter was sent to advise me how abusive the correctional institutions were. She gave some examples; she also referred to the failure of current programs and gave, as evidence of her position, the high recidivism rate. She concluded her letter with the statement that she was involved in a campaign "to clean things up."

I was well aware of Ms. Fonda's concerns over Viet Nam and her willingness to speak out for what she believed; however, it was not until I received her letter that I knew her thoughts about the treatment in prisons of blacks and other minorities. Her position must have been fresh in her mind and significantly augmented by personal experiences while on location in Louisiana in 1966. Her biographer, Fred Lawrence Guiles, recounts her support of movie director Preminger when he refused to accept the suggestion of the Ku Klux Klan that two of her co-stars, both black, stay in a rundown local hotel suitable for "niggers" and not be allowed to use the "white" swimming pool.

Ms. Fonda understood the concerns of the Black Panthers. Although her letter to me was not identified as a part of the Black Panther Movement, the general tenor of the presentation and the message delivered was identical to that which the Black Panther representative had conveyed to me.

I feel certain her letter had wide distribution among correctional officials across the country.

Although I was aware of the abuses about which she wrote and could have added much to her writing, I found her letter troublesome. It carried the connotation that there was a hurry to bring about the changes which signaled to me the distinct possibility that it might produce dramatic resistance at a very sensitive moment in the Reform Movement. Legislatures bow to public pressure and all the Washington Legislature would have had to do was to ordain that the Reform Movement in Washington was at an end and all the good efforts of so many would have come to an abrupt end.

I was pleased that the need for change was getting such broad recognition, but deeply concerned that too much change in too much of a hurry — accompanied by the inevitable anger such bad conditions had stimulated — would be met by resistance and could lead to a curtailment of our activities in Washington State.

Several months after the Black Panther visit and the Fonda letter, I appeared on a University of Washington-sponsored panel as a respondent to an address by Thomas Murton, Director of Corrections in Arkansas. Much of what he said was pioneering and constructive. He, too, was shocked at the perpetuation of a traditional, failed approach in corrections.

In my response I took the position that one had to move cautiously and carefully in making changes because resistance to change was everywhere. I strongly supported the democratization of prisons but I felt one could never give away control of these institutions; the resident of the institution was there to learn — not to administer. In order to make the improvements we all hoped to see, we needed to move ahead methodically. The superintendent's veto power needed to be preserved. When the phrase "veto power" left my lips, a quartet in the rear of the auditorium began a chant: "Fuck your veto power!" (The apparent lack of spontaneity in their chorus left little doubt that their presence there and their dirge were well planned.)

On still another occasion, when I spoke to a group of residents at the Walla Walla institution, I discussed their responsibility as citizens within the correctional system and even while incarcerated they might participate in the democratic way of life that governed our country. I mentioned again, as I always did, that the superintendent had veto power. One of the more daring young black residents looked me in the eye as he calmly said, "Fuck your veto power!" I feared the uncontrolled and sometimes radical approach being advocated both inside and outside the institutions would impede the implementation of reform programs. Mine was a deliberate approach; I feared others might be in too big a hurry.

◊◊◊◊◊

From a variety of sources, both local and national, it appeared that unhappiness was afoot. Those who no longer had absolute control over the lives of others were rebelling. Organized labor felt it was losing some of its hold on its personnel and jobs. The "old guard" was simply refusing to move in a new direction. And advocates for the downtrodden were saying moderate reforms weren't enough.

Viewed from any perspective, the unrest was a bad omen.

5
THE CONTE ERA

I became Director of Institutions in September 1966. The transfer of authority was smooth and easily accomplished. I was well acquainted with the Department after seven years of participation in its programs, and I was particularly aware of the correctional field because this was the area in which Garrett Heyns and I sensed the greatest need for program improvement.

I had learned well what to expect. Heyns understood the personnel involved in correctional services. He looked to the day when those who spoke the language of fair treatment and compassion would put their words into actual practice. In addition, he knew that with communication between staff and residents a fundamental requirement, some correctional staff would have trouble. Many had been attracted to their positions because of personality characteristics calling for firmness and aloofness. Now the rules were changing and they were expected to be communicators with a positive attitude. They hadn't counted on this.

But, change was the order of the day in adult corrections, and changes had to come even if they caused discomfort to some. The positive steps accomplished during the Heyns Era needed to be enhanced and new and creative approaches had to be developed to protect the people's investment in their correctional services. For far too long, tax dollars had been poured into programs commemorating failure. This could no longer be tolerated: neither for taxpayers, who deserved to see their money going into sound investments, nor for the residents of the institutions for whom the legislatures had created services aimed at helping them leave the institution as better people, not as more hardened criminals than when they entered.

It is pertinent to recall that in those times, the public was not as intolerant of crime and criminals as it is today. With public attitudes more favorable toward the disadvantaged, as was demonstrated in both the Rosellini and Evans administrations, we could count on considerable public support for the often neglected corrections field.

I suspect no politician in the 1980s could win an election based on campaign promises to rehabilitate criminals. While giving too little attention to the causes and prevention of crime, the general public is less interested in helping offenders live more fruitful lives. The fact that the current public attitude is not in the public's own best interest is a matter easily overlooked. While victims are, quite correctly, receiving more attention, that doesn't require neglecting the offender.

I had been cautioned about resistance to change, and I saw it first-hand. When one staff person recalled an execution and noted with pride that the man being executed "was on the end of a rope in 22 seconds," I shuddered with disbelief that anyone representing the State of Washington could be pleased with such a distasteful accomplishment even though he was referring to a legal duty. And, when I heard the uncomplimentary adjectives used by staff in describing residents of the prisons, I again wondered if an attitude even of tolerance could be created, let alone one of acceptance and compassion.

I presume that the persistent use of the term "inmate," uttered with derision and contempt, gave a clue to the very basic hostility some staff held toward their charges. We were soon involved in a campaign to use the term "residents" in referring to committed felons. It was a great day when, much later, the media picked up that designation.

Of course, I was viewed as being soft on crime, liberal, permissive and idealistic. If asking for understanding of the residents was "liberal," I plead guilty.

In time I was able to delegate the duties of my former (mental health) position in the Department and to reassure myself of the competency in the leadership of the other divisions of the Department of Institutions.

This allowed me to devote more time to corrections, the area of "unresolved issues and unfinished business," as my predecessor had described it. During on-site visits to the institutions, I again sensed the distance between residents and staff and a class consciousness in which residents assumed a subservient and often humiliated, humble, and passive attitude toward staff. Many times staff communications with residents dripped with sarcasm while responses from residents reflected overt fear and painful submission.

Perhaps most unfortunate of all, it appeared the institution, with its rules calling for isolation of prisoners and locking them out of sight, was in operation to provide jobs for the staff rather than to address and treat the needs of the residents.

Attitudes in general were not conducive to the treatment of residents. There was no way the institutions could be viewed as serving the long range needs of the state. Offenders were off the streets, but what was happening behind the walls too frequently brought no real chance for a safer society after the individuals were released. Instead, there was a near guarantee that such treatment would lead to greater frustration, anger and more negative acting out.

A View of Washington Prisons In The Mid-1960s.

The best that could be said about Washington State corrections in the '50s and '60s was that the program was a great improvement over that which had been in operation in Washington and nationally over the preceding 100 years. The least that could be said was that the system was not as effective as it might have been yet it was being perpetuated dutifully into the future by many dedicated corrections people.

Many of the old timers in the field were sincere and caring people who felt they were making a significant contribution and they were. They were loyal to their leaders and trying hard. Others seemed not to perceive the significance of statistics which suggested there was much room for improvement.[13]

Many built-in structures from the past made the life of prison officials everywhere rather comfortable. The warden was known to have a few key leaders among "his inmates." These persons served the role of the modern-day associate superintendent or personnel person. They were sometimes rewarded by special favors. They had choice cells, sometimes special privileges regarding food and work assignments and, of far greater importance, they enjoyed open and easy access to the superintendent. This gave the "chosen few" inmates a sense of prestige and power over their fellow residents of the institution.

These few were of great assistance to the warden. If there was trouble brewing, the warden learned about it through the "assistant superintendent" in prison garb. And, if there was a problem that needed attention, all the warden needed to do was advise his "associate behind the walls" of his expectations. This practice, although unconscionable in its unfairness to other residents, was generally followed in prisons throughout the country.

The management of prisons as recently as the '50s and '60s provided at times both unfair administration of justice and unequal application of the rules. This sparked the development of resentful individuals and groups within the institution with unrest and anger among the residents. It was totally counter-therapeutic.

Individuals who were received in the institutions came in on "the chain," i.e., literally handcuffed to a metal leash. Immediately upon arrival they were required to bathe in open showers. Deprived of their clothes and even the dirt on their backs, these men were quickly shown they had been banished from their past and had entered into a new arena—one in which their human status did not matter and where they were subservient to the power of individuals and groups that surrounded them. Certainly, neither the bill-paying citizens nor the Legislature anticipated there would be such disrespect shown to those who were being sent to the institution for rehabilitation.

In my early-day study of prison reform, I found encouragement in an article written by Superintendent B.J. Rhay published in *Perspective* in May-June 1960. Speaking on the matter of classification of "inmates," he stated:

> Few areas within the confines of the institution are more important to the inmate population than those particular areas which are included in the philosophy of classification ...(classification) affects each person in this institution perhaps more significantly than any other phase of the corrective formula...

> Classification is the gateway to the institutional program. It is the one place where the individual inmate meets with institutional staff members who are fully aware of all information relative to the individual, so that they can discuss particular problems with an eye toward developing a sound plan for the inmate to use as his guide throughout his imprisonment. This must be a plan that will lead the inmate through the front door and out into the free world better equipped to handle the problems of successful parole. It should be regarded as the arena of understanding, from the staff's standpoint as well as the standpoint of the inmate.

> Classification means...determining his (the resident's) special problems, and prescribing his custodial care, work program, education, vocational training, medical treatment, etc...which will be best suited to the prisoner. Each inmate's progress is checked periodically...

> Through classification, an individual program can be developed for each offender. p.8

The encouragement I received in reviewing articles such as this was at times short-lived. While sound in theory, in reality the classification procedure scarcely gave the impression that the institution was trying to determine the resident's special problems or attempting to find his greatest potential for work or training. Instead, the primary interest seemed to be that of satisfying the needs of the institution and the extent of his escape risk.

Classification "hearings" took place in a simulated courtroom. This consisted of a head table at which were seated certain prison officials. Inside the door (entering from the hallway) was a small table with no chair behind it. As the new resident came into the room, he stood behind the table to hear what "classification" had been decided upon. He made no comments and was given no opportunity to express himself. There was no chance for the resident to declare a willingness to cooperate or to relieve himself of any upset feelings which he might harbor. In fact, generally, when the resident entered the room, his presence was not recognized by even a nod from those at the head table. He stood more or less at attention in this militaristic atmosphere while those at the head table briefly ruffled through some papers. I was not impressed with the thoroughness of their study nor even with the possibility of there having been some prior perusal of the person's records. Ultimately, a decision was rendered: he would be placed under a certain degree of security.

But there was hope. The article by B.J. Rhay made it quite clear that the institution leadership understood the classification procedure and supported it.

Assignments for institution jobs were made in a way similar to the classification procedure. The decision-makers looked over a list of "openings" — jobs that needed to be done to keep the institution operating; again, the person was given no opportunity to express himself. Instead, he was told that he would work on the farm, do custodial work, or whatever else needed to be done. Unfortunately, practices of this sort let people highly skilled in one field work in another where they had no expertise and, perhaps, no interest. The entire procedures of classification and job assignment simply set the stage to augment the frustration that the individual already felt.

Once the decisions had been announced, the door behind the resident was opened and he was ushered out. The entire procedure took only a few minutes; no time was "wasted" in hearing from the subject of the meeting who was supposed to be in the institution to be rehabilitated.

Quite obviously, people do not go to prison for a vacation! Even so, I could never believe that the general public would be displeased with any honest and considered effort to help rehabilitate the resident. What I saw was a host of activities that tended to depreciate the resident and intensify his angry feelings. The resident was certainly not being helped.

Visits by family and friends were often the source of further frustration. Residents of the correctional facilities were not allowed to hold their children because it was thought that a revolver might be delivered to the resident via the diaper of the infant held in arms. More often than not, there seemed to be a desire to consider the disallowance of a supportive kiss from the resident's spouse as a part of the individual's punishment. At times, husbands and wives were not even allowed to touch each other.

Every resident in a correctional setting has a multitude of problems, some of which can only be handled by persons in authority. Obtaining an audience with a high level official was theoretically possible; however, the wait to see that official could be a matter of weeks or months, further manifesting the reality that the resident's concerns were not important.

From a therapeutic point of view, one other practice tended to neutralize whatever good was accomplished. Every incident, every utterance, and even the content of every counseling session could be presented to the Parole Board. One could count with certainty on the fact that any unpleasant comments would be forwarded. This meant that the person in prison had no opportunity to give vent to his feelings lest those feelings be held against him. It further meant a complete destruction of any therapeutic gain from whatever counseling was available. Not to be able to speak freely to the counselor and know that confidentiality would be preserved meant that negative feelings were held in, and those suppressed emotions remained to find expression in further antisocial behavior later.

Perhaps the most desperately dehumanizing situation I encountered was that of the strip cells and their utilization. As their name implies, men who had violated a rule or who had displeased a guard were placed in these cells without their clothes. The cells were generally small; they had one light, which was turned off for all but a few minutes of every day.

The individual incarcerated in the cell was visited only when "it was time to feed." The normal physiological activities were cared for through a hole in the floor which, to be unpleasantly frank, did not have flushing facilities. Men incarcerated under such conditions were sometimes kept there for weeks at a time. Their spirits were broken.

It would be difficult to define the extent of the problems incorporated in the prison system in the sixties. The practices had been hallowed for such a long time they were viewed as acceptable and even helpful by those who imposed them on their fellow human beings, their charges, their brothers.

One could go on and on describing the inadequate and unkempt physical plants, the lack of adequate medical attention (one woman in need of a hysterectomy waited six weeks for emergency surgery), the inappropriate supervision of female residents by male guards, and so on. Suffice it to say here that conditions in the prisons were dehumanizing and unreasonable. They set the stage for little positive learning or any other form of treatment endeavor.

Individuals in prison in the time about which I write had no telephone contact with their families, had their hair cut short whether they liked it or not, knew their mail might be censored, and had essentially no say in what was happening to, for, or about them. They stepped through the prison doors to become numbers and to lose their identities as human beings.

The Heyns message concerning humane treatment was echoed in some quarters. But, it may have been an attempt to win favor by espousing the "party line" rather than an honest expression of a deep desire on the part of correction staff to reach out to their charges and to help them change.

If one applied the family test and asked whether or not one would be comfortable knowing a beloved member of his or her own family was being cared for in the state's correctional facilities at the time, the answer would be an emphatic NO!

◊◊◊◊◊

The new administration set out in the fall of 1966 to further the change from punishment to treatment. The implementation of the efforts extended to that point in time merely set the stage for more progressive developments and a broader participation by all staff.

In an effort to more fully define the goals of the Reform Movement and to provide guidelines, I developed a position paper entitled *A Philosophy of Corrections.*

The paper was reacted to and modified by individuals both within and outside the corrections programs. It was publicly announced, frequently referred to and illustrated in a vast array of conferences, seminars and formal presentations.

For practical reasons, an outline of the Philosophy was prepared. This abbreviated form is reproduced here in its entirety with only minor editorial changes.

A Philosophy of Corrections.

Department of Institutions, Division of Adult Corrections. A Summary —

I. *Purposes and Goals:*

A. Correctional programs were created by society for the protection of society, the prevention of crime, and for the rehabilitation and successful re-entry of offenders into society. Although practical problems and conflicts among these diverse objectives do arise, society has every right to expect that these objectives will be met.

B. The fact that actual programming within the correctional program is left in the hands of professional rehabilitationists, educators, therapists and experienced correctional personnel creates maximum opportunity for initiative and creativity in program development.

C. The time during which a client is assigned to a correctional endeavor must be held in sacred trust by correctional staff. Every effort must be extended to assist the client in using it wisely and profitably.

D. Everything done to, for, or about an individual must have as its primary purpose the successful return of that individual to productive and responsible citizenship.

E. The primary objective of all correctional efforts is the client's return to responsible citizen participation employing a pattern of behavior which is both rewarding to the individual and acceptable to society.

II. *Nature of the Problem in Corrections:*

A. Human behavior is never independent of the conditions under which it occurs. In seeking the causes of, and remedies for, a particular client's actions, it is always necessary to consider as comprehensively as possible the full range of circumstances within and around the individual which have, in combination, given rise to the action. The individual offender cannot be adequately understood without reference to the totality of his/her experience.

B. The hope that the problems of the offenders may be solved by treating them in isolation or in any single unit of the corrections program is a false hope. A total array of services is mandatory.

70

III. *Nature of Rehabilitative Services:*

A. Evaluative and rehabilitative services must be comprehensive, i.e., they must be concerned with the total person — his/her physical and emotional health; social contacts and relationships, values and attitudes, weaknesses and strengths, capacity for meaningful employment, and opportunity for social, recreational, religious, and philosophical pursuits.

B. Rehabilitation (personal, social, vocational, etc.) is a growth process. Programs calling for varying and increasing degrees of maturity, capability, responsibility, and independence must be provided.

C. An effective habilitation and/or rehabilitation process demands an array of services, including: (1) evaluation and treatment, (2) probation, (3) protective institutional care with community involvement in comprehensive programming, (4) pre-release services and (5) continuing care in parole guidance.

D. The fact that correctional programs must deal with substantial numbers of clients requires an emphasis upon group techniques, but these must be developed in such a way that individual needs are met. Necessary opportunities for individualized care and attention must also be preserved.

E. Personal counseling, academic and vocational training; social, religious and recreational opportunities must be available in every phase of the corrections program.

F. Counseling services should be directed toward the problems of the client — personal, family, vocational, etc. The counselee, as counselees in other settings, has a *right* to confidentiality.

G. Pre-parole services, work and training release, and furlough programs directed toward the support of the individual in his/her readjustment to family, community, job, etc.

H. Parole services must be multi-purpose. They must (a) provide aid to the individual in establishing him/herself as a constructive member of society, (b) accommodate the statutory requirements, (c) assist in the protection of society, (d) extend opportunities for personal growth via individual and/or group processes, (e) provide the individual with a supportive bridge from his/her release from confinement to his/her achievement of an adequate vocational, personal, and social adjustment.

IV. The Climate of Correctional Programs:

A. Correctional institutions, while inevitably an artificial environment, must be oriented to community life. Programs must provide the resident access to work and training opportunities, health and social services, recreational and religious pursuits, etc. This can be aided substantially by citizen participation in every phase of institutional life.

B. All reasonable efforts must be made to avoid or overcome the disabling effects of institutionalization.

C. Treatment, facilities, earned wages, personal recognition, etc. all convey the message of worth to an individual client. Thus, these elements of correctional programs must be of high quality and always oriented to the support of the dignity of the human being for whom they have been created.

D. An individual must be treated by all correctional staff in a manner consistent with that which he/she is expected to employ or with which he can be expected to be treated after his release.

V. Rules and Discipline:

A. It is scarcely necessary to emphasize that residents of correctional institutions, like all citizens, are responsible to the laws of the State and Nation, and that the adherence to the rule of law expected of citizens-at-large applies equally to citizens-in-confinement.

B. Correctional programs should encourage each individual to make judgments and behave responsibly rather than relying exclusively upon rules to tell him/her what he/she should and should not do. Expectations of maturity, judgment, personal initiative, responsibility and respect for the rights, property, and well-being of others should be conveyed positively in every way possible.

C. Such general "house rules" as are necessary to maintain orderliness and constructive patterns of behavior in group living situations should be reasonable, clear, well communicated to residents, and should be reviewed periodically to evaluate their relevance, fairness, and practicality. Whenever feasible, resident members should participate in the formulation and evaluation of these guidelines.

D. Where actual penalties are attached to infractions, the rules must be fully explained and defined, with clearly understood consequences for violations, and careful attention to "due process" included in their administration. Flexibility necessary to apply the rules to fit the situation must be retained and the limits of this flexibility also made clear.

E. Punitive measures administered in the correctional system must always be relevant, appropriate, and should employ the least possible force necessary to bring the situation under control. Penalties must never be cruel, unusual, or excessive, and should never be administered in anger.

F. Disciplinary staff should be carefully selected and trained for their ability to set a strong and dependable example of patience, consistency, firmness, objectivity, and self-control.

G. Corrections should rely on punitive measures only after other avenues of influencing behavior have failed.

H. Cooperation should be viewed as a mutual responsibility of clients and staff. Resisting the temptation to simply place blame, each should seek ways to resolve differences and reduce struggle. While order must be maintained, it should always be recognized that lasting changes in attitude and behavior are far less likely to emerge from obedience than from respect.

VI. *Family Resources and Services:*

A. Whenever available, potentially capable, and willing, families can provide a great source of support to the residents in correctional programs and to parolees. Their understanding and help should be cultivated.

B. Recognizing the importance of families to the morale of correctional clients, all reasonable efforts should be made to assist their families with problems which arise in the course of an individual's assignment to correctional programs.

VII. Education and Research:

A. Probably no single element of the correctional program is more important than the knowledge, experience, and skill of its staff. Opportunities for staff education and development should be expanded and participation in educational pursuits vigorously encouraged and supported.

B. There is an ever-present need for research in the corrections field. We must become increasingly involved in replacing opinion with knowledge.

C. While correctional programs are addressed primarily to rehabilitation, educational and research efforts should embrace a wide range of subject matter from the prevention of crime to the successful return of ex-offenders to community living.

6
FURTHER IMPLEMENTATION OF REFORMS

With the adoption of a philosophy around which corrections staff could coordinate their efforts, the stage was set for further implementation of the changes Freeman and others had called for in 1957: ineffective punitive measures were to be replaced by "careful diagnosis and treatment..." p.26

The plan to implement the program after 1966 incorporated the following steps:

I. A continuing recital of the Philosophy of Administration and the coordination of efforts to clearly spell out the desire of leadership to carry out that philosophy,

II. Problem identification and solving calling for individual and group study of certain problems and issues and documentation of findings related thereto. (Problems such as standards for evaluation, readiness for parole, family needs, etc. were to be reviewed.)

III. Legislative action and administrative developments,

IV. Training of staff,

V. Four major reforms.

Each of the above steps is elaborated upon in the pages that follow.

I.   Philosophy of Administration

Early in 1967, I restated my desire, as the Director of Institutions, that all staff be involved in program definition, planning and implementation.

A statement of the Department's Philosophy of Administration was widely circulated. This position clearly noted that the composite thinking of all interested staff was likely to result in the best decision making, and staff at all levels had the opportunity to learn about and share ideas, anywhere, anytime. The emphasis on the Philosophy of Administration clearly defined the dedication of the Department to this method of communicating and operating.

II.   Problem Identification and Solving

Many topics suggested by staff at all levels of the administrative structure and (deemed) necessary for study were "put up for grabs," that is, volunteers were recruited to come together for study and planning. Sometimes, when there were no "takers" for such endeavors, groups were called together and asked if they would participate. Some delightful developments resulted from this approach.

For example: One group outlined the basic information necessary and prepared guidelines for correctional and parole decisions. Previously, there was no centrally located depository of information, nor were there current outlines as to what kinds of information were required for such decisions, or how to report them. Guidelines were developed for pre-sentence investigation, also a responsibility of the Department of Institutions.

Another ad hoc group rewrote manuals on Department procedures related to corrections, with the Philosophy of Administration and treatment of the offender in mind. These materials detailed policies, procedures and practices in corrections as well as the goals for rehabilitation of the offender.

Among the more important steps taken was the regular scheduling of meetings for the superintendents of the correctional institutions and certain of their staffs. An effort was made at each meeting to schedule the next and to have some discussion as to what the agenda for the next session should be. This gave ample time for study of the agenda and for superintendents to consult with members of their staffs at the institutions. The scheduled sessions occurred (about) every third month.

Agendas for these sessions in the beginning were easily dealt with; they were not likely to be upsetting. But the thoughtful attendee had no difficulty in perceiving that change was in the making. Some topics from these agendas are quite revealing:

A.   Review of material required for correctional and parole decisions. The resulting material ultimately was published in booklet form in August 1970; it outlined pre-sentence investigations, adult correctional admission summary, progress reports, release referral, pre-parole investigations, etc.;

B.   Criteria for granting minimal custody;

C.   Training needs for custody and treatment staff;

D.   Due process in transfers;

E.   Medical services and how to improve them;

F.   Length of stay at the Reception Center;

G.   Mail regulations;

H.   Training aid programs;

I.   Use of volunteers in correctional institutions;

J.   Multiservice centers with volunteer staff;

K.   Classification procedures;

L.   Revamping classification procedures;

M.   Resident Councils;

N.   Special programs for residents in death row; and

O.   Education for residents below the high school level.

Each agenda item was carefully chosen to serve the Reform Movement or could be easily converted to such an endeavor. For example, to talk of mail regulations was certain to call for a discussion of the lack of privacy and the sense of disrespect that must have been felt by every resident of a correctional facility. To revamp classification procedures was to make clear the need to involve residents in the planning of their prison careers. To discuss training of staff gave many opportunities for staff to consider why difficult-to-understand behavior might have an explanation and could possibly become understandable. To consider medical services and educational resources provided an opportunity to illustrate that prisoners are people who have a right to receive medical care and to improve themselves educationally.

As with my predecessor, I extended every effort to implement the basic principles so important in changing the ineffective prison record: humane treatment, an understanding of people and why they get into trouble, and constructive approaches to bringing about personality changes.

III. Legislative Action and Administrative Developments

The following notations refer to changes made in the latter half of the 1960s. The order of their being accomplished is not entirely preserved here due to an idiosyncrasy within the governmental process in which appropriations sometimes precede authorization, and vice versa.

The comments here are (generally) taken from the materials used in communications with the staff, the Legislature and the general public as each statute was discussed.

A. *Furloughs.* The staffs had reported with increasing frequency that certain residents were experiencing difficulty in maintaining their personal identity and perpetuating their influence with family and community. Further, it was always known that the sudden transfer from prison resident to community participant at the time of parole presented many problems. The furlough authorized on the basis of need for those who had demonstrated their readiness for such privileges corrected this deficiency for the resident and greatly enhanced his opportunity to adjust at home.

B. *Pre-Sentence Evaluation.* These evaluations were made mandatory. Under existing law, pre-sentence evaluations were performed only when staff was available to provide the review. By making them mandatory, funds *had* to be found, thereby assuring that the State's judges would have available this valued information concerning those who came before them.

C. *Work Release.* In a measure passed in 1967, the Department (at first with the consent of the parole board) was authorized to allow a resident of an institution to take leave of the prison campus for work and school. As a result, the resident could possibly make some dollar contributions to the care of his or her family or continue to move toward academic goals or vocational ambitions while still serving the required sentence.

D. *Gate Money.* Under existing law at the time, a person leaving prison was entitled to "suitable clothing, transportation to the place designated in his parole plan, and the sum of forty dollars" (RCW 72.08.343). With appropriate legislative action, this grossly inadequate amount was changed to one hundred dollars. Still not enough money to get started on, but twice as good as before the Legislature changed it!

E. *Removal of Restrictions on the Number of Chaplains in Any One Institution.* Following this legislation, the decision as to how many chaplains were needed in any program was decided by the Director of the Department of Institutions rather than by the Legislature.

F. *Agreements With Local Schools.* By this statutory authority, the Director was authorized to enter into agreements with school districts and institutions of higher learning for the use of their physical facilities and/or to allow the use of an institutional facility by a school. The local school superintendent was, of course, always welcome to bring a course of study with him!

G. *Work Release Housing.* The Department of Institutions was authorized by the Legislature to supervise work releases in designated and approved community housing across the state thus extending the scope of opportunities for work releasees beyond the community in which the prison was located.

H. *Interstate Compact on Detainers.* The passage of this agreement between the states, while setting the stage to transfer residents from one political jurisdiction to another with greater ease, had far greater significance in that it enabled residents to gain credit for time served while on leave to resolve legal charges against them in other states.

I. *Mental Health Program at the State Penitentiary.* Additional nursing staff and a part-time teacher were added to develop after-care units in the correctional facility, providing care for persons no longer in need of 24-hour psychiatric hospitalization but who were not yet able to function successfully in the general prison population. (This program served 500 persons each year.)

J. *A Contract for Services With the Division of Vocational Rehabilitation.* This contract called on DVR to evaluate, support, and train residents from the correctional institutions during and after their confinement. At long last, practical work opportunities could be planned for persons leaving prisons.

K. *Letters of Understanding With Community Colleges.* This program enabled colleges near the institutions to conduct courses on the institution campuses and permitted residents to attend courses in community colleges when on work release.

L. *Increased Community Involvement in Pre-Release Programs.* With the opening of the institution doors to the community, and as work release and furloughs became available to residents, there was a considerable exchange of treatment and teaching personnel with local communities. This measure authorized and enhanced the opportunity for residents to become involved in programs offered by job-finding organizations, business and finance consultants, and a host of other community based health, religious and social organizations.

M. *Transfer of Parole Staff.* Staff assuming parole responsibilities were transferred by the Legislature from the jurisdiction of the Parole Board to the Department of Institutions, thereby providing an opportunity to better coordinate pre-sentence evaluative services and discharge planning.

N. *Group Counseling in Parole Services.* Capitalizing on the knowledge and advantage of group therapy, counseling in groups was introduced into local parole offices. These services proved very helpful in aiding the parolee in his adjustment to home and community. It also tended to share valued clinical services with a larger group.

O. *Drug Abuse Treatment.* The 1969 session of the Legislature authorized the development of drug abuse treatment programs in all institutions. By the early 1960s, drugs had permeated every walk of life, and prisons were no exceptions. Drugs in correctional institutions were in particular demand, not only for the drug effect, but because they were powerful tools in the barter for materials and position.

P. *Volunteer Program for Parole Services.* Community volunteers were recruited for a host of services in parole offices across the state. These contributors ran the gamut from personal support services to professional counseling endeavors.

Q. *Services to Families.* This undertaking called for the development of support groups to assist spouses of incarcerated individuals with personal problems while their loved ones were in prison. Keeping families intact helped provide the resident a support system while he was incarcerated and enhanced his potential for successful reentry into community life.

The Corrections Center for Women.

In 1966, the people of the State of Washington made available by referendum sufficient monies to develop a new correctional facility for women. The message had been heard: the Walla Walla structure was inadequate, depressing, and not conducive to treatment; and, the southeastern region of the state *was not a* good area for work release and training because of its isolation and limited resources. Thus, the Reform Movement was handed another opportunity to illustrate the advantage of humane treatment.

The Legislature appointed a committee composed of several members of the Legislature and the Director of Institutions to select the site for the new institution.

Senator George Kupka of Pierce County was chairman. The committee was well informed, operated as a team, and site selection got off on time. The Shelton institution, opened in November, 1964, had been well received and the committee hoped the new endeavor would be as creative. The location of the new program was of utmost importance.

High on the list of priorities which the committee identified was a location where there would be easy access to community services, schools, and work opportunities.

The state-owned land in Seattle, adjacent to the Fircrest School, would have been an excellent location although it was doubtful there was adequate space for the new program. Nonetheless, a trial balloon was flown to see what the public attitude might be toward a correctional facility in an inner city neighborhood. The answer was not long in coming: it would not be well received.

A number of other locations were suggested and each was given consideration. Several were ruled out because getting to them was very difficult. Even so, the committee visited each suggested site to be sure nothing was overlooked. One such safari required a jeep ride!

Finally, Senator Kupka suggested an area near Purdy. His home district was Tacoma and he was well acquainted with the location. He and I made the first visit to the property alone because there was no road — not even a clearing! He felt bringing the whole committee there was not warranted until I had seen it. Our journey was accomplished on a Sunday morning: it was raining and we were attired in hip boots, which proved to be absolutely essential for this particular exploration. I was immediately struck with the site! It was beautiful. The trees were tall and thick, creating privacy for those who would be housed there. They would not have to feel they were on display to the public passing by.

This was a large parcel of land, much more than would be needed. But, best of all, the Purdy location was close to Tacoma and Bremerton, and to two universities and two vocational schools so there would be many opportunities for on-the-job training and work experiences. My fantasy at the moment of first sight was that the State would buy vans and run its own busline for residents utilizing work-and-training-release. I am glad to report this dream became a reality.

When it came time to vote on the site location, there were a few pork barrel votes cast, but the handwriting was on the wall. A second vote resulted in the unanimous vote for Purdy.

In due time, the property was purchased and the architects were assembled. Working with a large group of correction staff and Ms. Edna Goodrich, then superintendent of the juvenile institution at Grand Mound and designated to become the first superintendent of the new facility for women, the leadership established the essential characteristics of the new endeavor. Specifically, the women's institution:

1. Should not look like a penal institution; instead, it would have a campus-like appearance.

2. There would be no wall. A fence would give proper respect to tradition, but should be unobtrusive and established in such a way that it could be easily removed; if the staff could acquire sufficient expertise in dealing with the character-disordered women who would come to be cared for in this new program, the fence would not be necessary.

3. Maximum security would be accomplished within the institution and it would be sufficiently tight to restrain the most recalcitrant resident and, at the same time, offer adequate protection to society.

4. The beauty of the grounds should be preserved. Privacy was an important aspect of the effort to avoid humiliation for the resident.

5. Private rooms were a must, as was a courtyard for strolling or visiting. Adequate space for study, crafts, dining, and religious services was essential.

6. Apartments would be developed outside the institution compound which would provide an incentive for the resident to move toward a more responsible self-initiative. Those apartments would have facilities for cooking, cleaning, home care, etc., to be used in teaching the large number of women who did not already have home-making skills.

7. There needed to be easy access for getting cars, vans and busses in and out of the institution to facilitate the utilization of community resources in the rehabilitation process.

Every point in these specifications was debated. Some suggested that a prison wall would be necessary to prevent escapes. After all, they argued, a wall painted white caused the escaping "inmate" to be silhouetted and a good target from the gun tower. But, this position was quickly discounted when it was pointed out that the women's facility in Walla Walla had no wall around it and at Purdy there would be no gun towers! A number of persons suggested that a "nice" facility would cost more money and the public was not willing to make the expenditure. The architects were admonished to keep costs down, and they responded reassuringly that decent structures could have security built into them without additional costs.

Some objected to the trees surrounding the new institution and suggested the land should be cleared. Escaping residents would hide behind the trees and be difficult to apprehend. Others countered that there was an abundance of therapeutically-oriented individuals in the area from which to develop a cadre of treatment staff. And, as Edna Goodrich was to repeat on many occasions, "We are all learning how to handle difficult-to-handle people." It was hoped that, with treatment for the troubled resident and improved skills in the staff, escapes would be few in number.

Still others warned that the idea of placing residents in the communities would not be well received. They were reminded that there is resistance to every new idea, and program builders had to live with that.

Many suggested that if the institution was too nice, women leaving the pleasant surroundings would become depressed when they had to return to their own, more humble homes.

Again, the response was that a goal of treatment was to instill a sense of inspiration and hope in the resident; without experiencing something more favorable, how could one ever strive to acquire an improvement in her own living and working situation?

The Corrections Center for Women became a reality in late 1970. The Walla Walla experience for women could now be relegated to the past. Women in prison could come to a decent place with clearcut possibilities for rehabilitation. The vans worked, and so did work release! Security was maintained in one unit of the institution that looked like all the rest of the structures so those not needing such close supervision did not have to be confronted with the daily reminder of their classification.

Another vital step in prison reform had been launched.

IV.   Training.

To further the goal of giving each staff member some working concept of the development of pathological behavior, sociologist Tom Adams was appointed to develop and lead an educational program for correctional staff and parole officers. Coming to Washington from The

Western Interstate Commission on Higher Education, he joined the program in 1967.

Adams felt the best way to approach his objective with staff would be to create a training program in the community through which most, if not all of the staff might rotate for a real-life ghetto experience.

There they could meet the disadvantaged, spend time looking at the physical and financial hardships under which they labored, and experience the hand-to-mouth existence so characteristic of many of the residents who came to be under the care of the Department of Institutions.

Interest was high, movement rapid, and soon after his arrival a continuing series of sessions were held in the Frye Hotel in downtown Seattle, which became a new "study campus" for staff in the field of corrections. This endeavor is best described in an article written for *Perspective* in the winter of 1970 by John Peterson, a journalist-participant in the program. Peterson described the experience of "a man from the Frye" who was "turned loose" from the State Penitentiary with forty dollars in gate money. Peterson, the "man from Frye." finds that:

> Prison nomenclature has changed over the years; you're a 'former resident' now instead of an 'ex-con,' you've been in an 'adult correctional facility' instead of a prison, and the fellow who drops you off at the Greyhound depot is a correctional officer instead of a guard.

> But the gate money hasn't changed. The amount was set by statute so long ago that forty dollars could, with careful management, permit a man to survive for a month.

> It won't any more. The man in the Seattle skid road hotel room could testify to that. Half the allotted sum had gone to pay a week's rent on the dreary room he occupied. He had grown used to the threadbare carpet...but not to absolute poverty itself. It is only the fourth morning, and the forty dollars are gone. Shaving in cold water in the unheated bath-room, the man brushed his single suit, and then his shoes, with a ragged towel, then took the creaking elevator down to street level to face the world...the grimy, garish skid road world of society's rejects.

> A breakfast of coffee and doughnuts in a basement cafe was paid for with the last of the small change from the vanished forty dollars.

It was time to hit the street…to stand in the long lines at the state employment office and learn that jobs may be available for computer processors, marine architects and experienced heavy equipment operators, but not for a former maker of license plates.

The man from the Frye Hotel was living an experience common to thousands of other men who are low priority employment prospects because of prison records and lack of training.

But there was one unique difference. Tomorrow he would stop being a two-time loser. He would check out of the Frye Hotel, drive to the state capital and resume his real life as a member of the State Board of Prison Terms and Paroles.

…Designed by a group of academic sociologists, the program has a dual goal:

The first is to make society and the people who man its institutions that deal with the down-and-out…the courts, prisons, police, and parole apparatus…more flexible and understanding of the problems and feelings of society's losers.

The institute's second aim is to take as much of the rehabilitation process as possible out of the institutions and away from the bureaucrats and put it in the community where the convict and victim come from…

Trainees have included adult and juvenile parole officers, correctional officers, counselors, chaplains, social workers, and administrators of the sponsoring agency, the Division of Institutions, along with policemen, college instructors, court officials and representatives of other governmental social and health service agencies. All live for five days at the Frye Hotel, where the institute maintains its headquarters. All are expected to maintain themselves on the forty dollars provided by the state to released parolees…

Superintendent Rhay Goes to Europe.

Under a grant from the Leckenby Foundation, Seattle, it was possible to arrange a European study program for Bob Rhay, Superintendent of the Washington State Penitentiary. He left Seattle on April 14, 1970. Mr. Rhay outlined the purpose of his trip in the Planning Prospectus, a publication of the Division of Corrections, he says:

It was agreed in the formative phase of this project that the basic purpose of the tour would be to study the newest ideas and practices in the correctional field in a number of selected institutions in Western European nations. Consequently, the tour was arranged to examine ideas rather than bricks, concrete and steel of institutional architecture.

Among the most important objectives were:

1.   To study innovative techniques designed to increase the treatment effort;

2.   To gain an understanding of the use and development of community-based correction centers;

3.   To discover, if possible, the ingredients used in developing successful programs;

4.   To exchange ideas with leading European penologists and prison administrators; and

5.   To visit selected institutions. p.71

The travel took Mr. Rhay to England, France, The Netherlands, Denmark, Norway, and Sweden, the latter four countries for their progressive prison programs.

After commenting at length on staff selection (Rhay found many administrators of correctional programs in Europe to be young attorneys and law professors) and training, the smaller institutions he visited there, "visitors and advisors" for correctional residents, etc., he discusses decriminalization and democratization. Rhay notes that the countries he visited seemed to be taking steps to avoid the criminal designation as long as no one is offended. And, in regard to democratization, he writes:

One witnesses real feelings of humanity on the part of prison staff and inmates which seem to be genuinely based on an appreciation of human worth and dignity of the individual. Great credit for this must be given to the training process for prison personnel beginning at the time of employment and the immediate involvement of new staff with the offerings of the Staff Colleges.

He closes his report with the comment:

The warm rapport between staff and inmate on the European front indicates that the dignity of individual inmates can be maintained when staff is concerned.

These positive comments were interpreted as a plus in the Reform Movement. A time-honored leader in corrections had seen some positive advantages in a humane approach to offenders, and he had written about it! The trip had proven successful even while Rhay projected some of his own questions as to whether similar programs could be developed in the United States: The European's inbred respect for authority and professionalism makes it easier to impose new ideas. p.75

V.   Four Major Reforms

After years of intense effort on the legislative front, training sessions that seemed to know no end and meetings of staff at every level of the administrative structure, it seemed time to approach certain of the more abusive, destructive, (and probably unconstitutional) practices of the traditional prison. Four specific reforms were introduced, explored, and interpreted extensively before being announced publicly in November 1970 at a Discussion-in-Depth in Seattle. They were given national attention in the corrections field in an article published in The *American Journal of Corrections*, May-June 1971.

The reforms were:

1.   Abolition of the strip cell, which was blatantly the most dehumanizing of all practices at the time,

2.   Abolition of the censorship of mail which was illegal in the first place

3.   Establishment of the privilege of making private collect telephone calls to assist the individual in maintaining contact with those he left behind,

4.   Establishment of a Resident Governmental Council to allow residents a forum to express themselves and at the same time to learn something of what it means to participate in legal, formal, and proper representative expression of their interests and concerns. Action of the Resident Governmental Council was to be implemented only with the approval of the superintendent.

The first three of these reforms were clearly humanitarian in their orientation. They followed closely in the pattern of improved housing, food and medical attention, the availability of chaplains, gate money and furloughs — all movements with which the personnel in the prison system were well acquainted.

The fourth of the reforms was more structural in its orientation and was a highly specific educational effort. It seemed particularly practical for teaching a temperate approach to societal change for a population of individuals who for the most part had not been patient in making such changes. The reform also required teachers who were supportive of a democratic way of life…a characteristic totally foreign to prison life.

Shortly after the four specific reforms were announced, the total reform effort instituted by the Department received positive feedback in an editorial in the *Longview Daily News*, which commented upon the November press release:

> …Recognizing that prison is a harsh, dehumanizing, esteemless world, the State Division of Institutions wants to do something to change it.
>
> It is considering a variety of changes designed to restore some human dignity to incarceration and to better fit prison to the man rather than vice versa.
>
> Some of its proposals are elemental and should have been instituted long ago.
>
> For instance, it wants to require a presentence investigation of each convicted felon. Such reports give the judge background and analysis information which allows him to better understand the man before him…a majority of the proposals are new to Washington. They include:
>
> Allowing selected inmates furloughs of up to 72 hours for family visits or job interviews.
>
> Quick parole — after as little as six weeks in prison — for selected inmates who have completed diagnosis at the Shelton Corrections Center. For some men, one day in prison is enough…
>
> Stopping the censorship of most inmate mail but continuing supervision and limits on inmates correspondence… there is no reason officials should want to censor a man's mail. It is just one more device for removing a man's self-esteem and identity…
>
> The state's proposals are all worth instituting even if some might be on a limited basis at first. To be effective, incarceration must be as positive and progressive as possible. Inmates must have self-esteem and identity before they will be interested in bettering themselves.

Elaboration and Reaction (The Four Reforms).

To make clear the implications of the several reforms, I will summarize here some reactions from certain residents who shared with me their feelings in regard to these unhappy aspects of prison life.

Many correctional facilities had seemed not to grasp the significance of the fig leaf to Adam and Eve. Humans have always wanted to cover their nakedness. Toilet facilities without shields in the individual cells were humiliating enough. To force a person into dark isolation, without clothes and without facilities available on most campgrounds, did nothing but cause embarrassment and anger. The strip cells as a means of punishment were not effective: they served only to depreciate the personhood of the individual.

A few days after the strip cells were abolished, a prison official from one of the institutions called my office, asking what the prison could do (now that the strip cells would no longer be used) when a man got upset and "out of control." A very frustrated associate in my office suggested the official might try talking to the resident to find out what was troubling him.

A young man once showed me a letter he had received from his girlfriend. It had been censored. Words and even whole sentences had been clipped out of the letter, destroying the message censored, to be sure, but also removing the message written on the reverse side of the page upon which the letter had been continued. The woman had obviously been writing her tender thoughts because the general nature of the paragraph censored revealed her feelings of intimacy. The incensed young man asked me how it was that his lover's innermost thoughts interfered with the security of the prison or how they could possibly be interpreted as being destructive to his adjustment in the correctional setting. I was at a loss to answer.

Another time, I witnessed a resident opening a censored letter only to find it shredded by the censor to the extent that the message was not readable. He told me the letter was from his family — he knew this because he recognized the handwriting — but, there was scarcely an intelligible phrase left for him to savor.

The censored letter reminded me of a chain of paper dolls produced in child's play. Of course, not every letter could be censored. What of the information that got through because there weren't enough censors to go over every letter? And, even if the resident and his friends on the outside were planning a riot or an escape, would they have run the risk of revealing their intentions in letters, knowing that prison officials would have access to their plans? Most unlikely, I thought!

I viewed the censorship of mail as a violation of the privacy of the individual, as depriving him of open and direct communications with loved ones upon whom he would surely have to depend when he left prison.

Isolation from home and family responsibility produced great stress in the prisons. On many occasions I was told by residents that they had received letters referring to a sick child or an upset family member. They then suffered the torment of the damned, waiting for another letter to update their information. A telephone call would have put their minds at rest without further torture. Or, a word with a family member could have provided a moment of mutual support in the deadly loneliness of their separation. Although the resident was incarcerated as a result of his own actions, he had been handed no sentence calling for him to be driven psychotic by worry. Further, a word with family, as finances would permit, would have done much to preserve fragmented relationships and pave the way for reinstituting communication upon the resident's release.

The following letter from a resident in Monroe addressed to me as Director of the Department of Institutions clearly reveals the value of the changes made:

> Tonight, for the first time in 18 months, I wrote a letter that left me feeling good instead of frustrated. It's the first time since I've been here that I've felt free to write to her as myself.
>
> And it will be the first time since being here that she'll get a letter from the person she knows.
>
> I don't know what effect the new mail rules (or lack of them) will have on crime in the streets, drug abuse and the return rate to prison, but it will allow us to stay a little closer to our friends and families. They'll be getting letters from the men they know, not some stranger whose first concern is to NOT displease or offend a censor or counselor. It becomes a real drag after a while (if not immediately) to be a hypocrite and a liar with those you love in order to please someone who really doesn't even know you — or care to.
>
> It's really far out to have some personal life — again. Thanks!

The early reform efforts had met with little or no negative response from the keepers or the kept, and what resistance there was seemed to be of little consequence. No one objected to improvements in the physical plants. The residents of the institutions loved them, and the guards found improved facilities more pleasant places in which to work.

The improvements in medical services, although slow in coming and never adequate to meet the needs, were appreciated, although almost every improvement added to the recognition of how great the need really was.

A policy of transferring the more serious mentally ill residents to the state hospitals was met with wide acclaim. Work release and furloughs were warmly received also. The residents, of course, realized their advantage in each of these broad programs, and these reforms were no threat to the staff. Guards were convinced there would be no reduction in the total population — thus, no loss of jobs — since "the animals would goof up and be brought back."

Even the addition of teaching and counseling staff went forward without difficulty. There were clashes between "custodial" and "treatment" staff, but none of such magnitude as to threaten the effort to introduce treatment into what had often been warehousing institutions.

But, the specific reforms launched in November 1970, while acceptable to all but a very few residents of the institutions, met with another reaction on the part of staff accustomed to the custodial approach. Although communications on these new programs had been extensive, it was abundantly clear that many staff had difficulty understanding and accepting them. The fact that both my official and private mail on these topics increased tremendously gives testimony to the distress the new programs engendered.

Many staff were upset when they saw residents waiting in line to make collect phone calls. The feeling was expressed that these "inmates" had no real interest in their families; they had demonstrated by their offenses that they did not have such human qualities and were only planning escapes in their allegedly "calling home." Numerous obstructions were set up to prevent the calls from being made and calls often were interrupted for trumped-up reasons. In a number of instances, the same staff who had earlier protested physical contact between a resident and his family for fear a gun might be smuggled in were certain the phone privilege would be used to the disadvantage of the institution.

Similar fears were expressed in regard to relaxing the censorship of mail. Some believed there would be an influx of contraband into the institution.

The reminder that there was no limit on the search for weapons, drugs, or other unacceptable items in incoming mail seemed not to allay their fears.

The abolition of the strip cell also was resented deeply by some who unintentionally revealed that they dealt with their charges via force and threat, despite the hopes of the much-publicized Philosophy of Corrections and the trips to the Frye Hotel. And then came the Resident Governmental Council!

The Resident Governmental Council.

A great deal of attention was given to the Resident Governmental Council in the total Reform Movement. Some were to say that it was destructive rather than constructive. Without careful supervision and guidance and the use of the veto power when the ambitions of the Councils became unrealistic it could clearly not be in the best interest of the residents or the institution to have such a program. Uncontrolled councils could create the image of the organization as a governing body which, under the law, it could not be. Staff in such a situation would be powerless to carry out its responsibilities.

Because of its significance in the Reform Movement it is important that it be understood in detail. It is equally important that some of the preliminary thinking which went into its development be mentioned.

Garrett Heyns was impressed by the many failures experienced in the historical attempts to bring about prison reform. He had lived through them and knew from personal experience what such failures entailed and how traumatic they could be to the individuals involved. He always opted for the more conservative approach when it was necessary to take a new administrative step, so that the old guard might be induced to join in the changes.

There was always serious consideration given to the prison as a small community. Communities need to be governed and need structure through which the governing process may take place. In our society, we believe that the democratic approach calling for individual participation in the governmental process is the most effective structure. We are all better prepared to be governed when we are active participants in the governance. It stands to reason that prisons are better governed, and more peaceful, when residents are actively involved in the governing process.

It was clear to me that the reform of the prison system in Washington required the creation of a self government. This self government had to be fair, generally supported, appropriate and honest, if it were to be effective in teaching the institutions' residents the democratic and orderly approach to the rules and regulations of their society.

I felt self government could be accomplished in the prisons. However, I felt it should be developed at a pace the staff could accommodate.

It was equally clear that the Washington prison system was not ready in the late 1960s to engage in a broad democratic endeavor. Thus, it was decided to try a modest first step, with the hope that a matured acceptance of that preliminary endeavor would lead to more extensive democratization. That first step was the Resident Governmental Council.[14]

On November 6, 1970, the Office of Adult Corrections, Division of Institutions (of the newly-formed Department of Social and Health Services) circulated to the leadership in Adult Corrections the carefully-planned document establishing the Resident Governmental Council. The authorization for this reform clearly stated the purpose and hope of the program and reflected the results of the many conversations on the subject leading to the decision to proceed with this first step toward democratization of the prison system.

Because of its significance in the total reform effort, that memorandum is reproduced here in its entirety:

Department of Social and Health Services
Division of Institutions
Olympia, Washington
Office of Adult Corrections
Memorandum #70-7
Nov. 6, 1970

In order to prepare residents in the institutions for participation in life in the democratic society, it is important that in the institutions' society, opportunities for participation in democratic government be available. Participants in the institution society, as in the larger society, are better prepared to accept rules and regulations governing their behavior when they have been participants in the development of necessary rules and regulations.

The following listing incorporates the essential elements of resident government, which will be built into the residents' government in each of the correctional facilities if, indeed, these elements are not already present.

1.   Care will be taken to make certain that every resident in the institution has an identifiable representation in a resident governmental council. Regardless of the basis upon which representation is developed, each resident must be able to see clearly how (via

whom) he is represented in the council. Titles of representatives or governing bodies may vary from one institution to another.

2. Every resident shall have an opportunity to participate in the election of his representative. Representation may be based on housing units, or program areas, or other bases.

3. In order for the interests and wishes of the individual residents to be felt, organized forums will be developed within each of the units upon which representation is based. These forums will be required to meet at regular periods to ensure their activity.

4. The representation from the various units to the governmental council will be by open election and by secret ballot.

5. The resident governmental council will develop by-laws that will spell out terms of office, regulations of a procedural nature, methods of communication with the administration, etc. Elected representatives will be limited to one term of office.

6. The resident governmental council will present recommendations to the superintendent for his consideration. At the same time, the superintendent is at liberty to present recommendations to the resident governmental council for its consideration. The resident governmental council and the superintendent will provide notice, at least two weeks in advance, of items to be placed on the agenda, so that there will be ample time to study the matters to be scheduled for discussion at the meetings.

7. Private citizen participation will be insured by involving citizens representative of the larger community. Community representatives may meet individually with the superintendent, attend meetings of the resident governmental council and the council's meetings with the superintendent. The resident governmental council will be consulted prior to the designation of private citizens to participate with the resident governmental council and superintendent.

8. It is to be understood that the final responsibility and authority for the operation of an institution is vested, by law, in the superintendent. He will have veto powers. It is to be understood, further, that the exercise of that veto power will require great wisdom and will demand a clear supporting statement of why the veto has been found necessary.

9. Prior to adoption, the constitution and by-laws shall be submitted by the superintendent for approval of the Chief, Office of Adult Corrections.

10.   It is anticipated that the News Bulletin for adult corrections will report extensively on the activities of the resident governmental council.

A restatement of the principle of the Resident Governmental Council was incorporated in a progress report on this aspect of the Reform Movement and reported in the May-June, 1971 issue of *The American Journal of Corrections*. That report notes:

> A Resident Government organization has been established in each of the adult correctional institutions. This program calls for representation of the population on a Resident Council. Private citizen participation is also included in the Council operation.
>
> The primary purpose of the Council is to provide the resident of the institution with a formal channel of communication to the administration, an opportunity to present his hopes as well as his grievances in an orderly fashion, and to provide him with an experience in the implementation of the democratic philosophy. Off to a slow start because of differences of opinion concerning the constitution of the new organization's method of electing representatives, etc., the program has, nonetheless, been launched and has proven its usefulness. In any number of instances, the Resident Council has established rules, regulations and procedures which, after endorsement by the superintendent of the institution, have created a more harmonious institution. p.27

Special notice should be taken that the authorization reminded all parties of the superintendent's veto power and called for the superintendent's approval on actions of the Council. This was overlooked, denied, and in time, completely forgotten as anxiety over the program mounted.

The concept of the Resident Governmental Council arose from meetings and debates, both within and outside State corrections programs. It reflected a pressing desire to help residents understand the concept of citizen participation so that, upon leaving the institution, they might participate in society in an appropriate manner. Again, the burning question: is public safety enhanced when an individual, who is incarcerated for a period of time and then released more bitter than when he entered? Is not that individual likely to be a greater danger to society? Why not try to introduce residents to behavior that society considers appropriate, and hope they will acquire an interest in living as law-abiding citizens upon their release? The Resident Governmental Council held that promise. It was set up to give residents a feel for self-expression through the democratic process. With the superintendent required to approve of council actions, there should be no danger of things getting out of hand. Some residents strongly disliked the superintendent's veto power, but that could make no difference: he was given that authority by law.

The Council would provide for residents' representation in a body that could express its views, both positive and negative, to the administration. It would let residents in the institution know that even though they felt isolated, disenfranchised, and powerless, they had an avenue to the power structure governing their lives.

If the Resident Council did nothing more than serve as a forum for discussing frustrations and letting off steam, it would be useful. The 1960s will be remembered as the time of revolt and anger over the traditional ways of doing and getting, a time when free expression was the order of the day. Residents of correctional institutions already had much to be upset about.

We knew the Resident Governmental Council would always have an agenda filled to overflowing with angry complaints about bad conditions. Giving residents the opportunity to have a formal and organized way of expressing these feelings had to be a primary benefit of the Council. Having the chance to make constructive suggestions in problem solving could only be beneficial.

With the anger so great in the correctional institutions at the time, and with the hostile distance that existed between staff and residents, I felt that the Resident Governmental Council was absolutely necessary if a riot was to be averted. (In retrospect, I am certain Washington was spared an Attica because of the Reform Movement. I believe the difficult days in the mid '70s could have been avoided had the Movement been given an opportunity for full expression.)

Granted, the development of the Governmental Councils was a socio-academic reform which was not easy to implement. Coming together to think about democratic principles, representative government and orderly problem-solving were two groups of individuals who had never before given thought to such considerations within the prison system. The residents of the institutions could never believe anything in the prison would be other than dictatorial. Many of the guards had been attracted to their jobs in the first place because there were ironclad rules to be followed without deviation from the stated requirement.

Further, the differences between the groups involved were legion. Generally speaking, the men in prison had more legal experience than did their keepers and they were better prepared on constitutional issues after their extensive encounters with lawyers, courts and the appeal process. And the staff, with their background in high school civics, felt they had sufficient knowledge and understanding of the democratic process to qualify them for their roles as teachers of the "uninformed."

There were profound philosophical differences also. The average staff person often espoused a highly conservative point of view which was in direct conflict with the more liberal thinking of the institution resident.

It is no wonder that the residents working on council structure and the constitutions for the new program complained that there was no help from the staff. Many staff could not be of help. Many staff were uncomfortable as discussions ensued which were beyond their capacity to comprehend.

At no time was the Resident Governmental Council considered an instrument of power for residents, or a *self* government. In fact, "self government" would have been contrary to law. Nonetheless, the cry went out that "self government" had made the correctional facilities unsafe. Somehow the word "self" came to be inserted in the title, and it caught fire. Perhaps prior attempts at self government in other states led to a misinterpretation of the program. Those who did interpret the Resident Governmental Council as *self* government seemed to forget that the superintendent always held veto power over everything it did.

Still, that term, "*self* government," was to endure. It was picked up by the staff, their wives, the Legislature, and even a study panel of consultants who later were called in to study problems that followed the creation of the Department of Social and Health Services, an umbrella agency that included the Department of Institutions.

Of course, without the superintendent's veto power, the Resident Governmental Council would have amounted to self government. But I clearly did not believe the institutions were ready for self-government at that time and scrupulously avoided it.

I was to learn much later that rumors or unfortunate misinterpretations were rampant within the institutions. Some erroneous ideas seemed to spring forth from the very beginning of the Resident Governmental program. Some believed the Resident Council was to be a 50-50 partner in governing the institution at Walla Walla; they must have been supported in this belief when a resident of the institution was permitted to sit in on meetings of the administrative staff.

A former resident of the Walla Walla institution who had served sentences totaling more than fifteen years was asked (years later) what he thought about the reforms and particularly "self" government. He responded:

> ...I think it was designed to fail. It was implemented with no preparation.[15] One day, as we inmates behind the walls saw it, they said, "OK, there are no more rules; you have self government." Now, I didn't know what that meant — nobody did. But the guards, the correctional officers, they knew what it meant. It meant that the inmates now were in control of the joint...so they (the guards) were backing off...

Interesting, indeed, that an educational tool created to teach participation in government would be interpreted as a mechanism to transfer the governing authority to the resident population, regardless of the statutory requirements to the contrary.

One must wonder how such interpretations could arise.

The thought that the resident of the institution was to be in a position to have some input into his own care, and that he could make formal intercessions to the administration in an approved and organized manner, seemed more than some could bear. The residents could even voice complaints and do so in an arena that might receive public attention because of the presence of community representation in such "internal" negotiations.

I was disappointed, of course, that the training experiences and the position of the leadership had not been more effective. However, there is much to explain these reactions. To simplify, one need only to realize there were two distinct and clearly visible motivational modes among correctional officers: that of the non-career staff and that of those who planned to be long term employees.

Briefly stated, employment in the correctional field was not — and isn't — financially rewarding. Many who joined the staff were younger persons who held these low-prestige jobs only until they could complete their educations or start new businesses of their own. For them, the main effects of the four specific reforms were to consume more time and require more work than the usual, more restrictive programming. Making changes would require more effort than these short-term employees were willing to commit.

Meanwhile, the career staff, or the "old guard," felt emotionally attached to the line of work that had been pursued by their fathers and their fathers' fathers. They saw the handwriting on the wall; they feared that if these programs worked, and prisons became effective treatment institutions, their jobs might became obsolete.

Possible reductions of staff have always struck fear in the heart of organized labor, and apparently they still do. As recently as 1987, the Employees' Union went to court to prevent the transfer of 60 patients from Western State Hospital to a community-based placement because the transfer might reduce the number of jobs for mental hospital workers.

The fear expressed in the '60s is understandable; at that time there was no way to predict there would be a need for more staff to meet ever increasing crime rates. Also, at that early date organized labor did not realize the position of power they were to receive as a result of the creation of the Department of Social and Health Services.

The fears of the staff were augmented almost daily. The residents were invited — in fact, they were encouraged — to become involved in the Resident Governmental Council and they accepted the opportunity in good spirit, cooperatively and industriously. Committees of the Resident Governmental Council went to work developing the "constitutions" for the new councils, and there was an air of business around the institutions.

Many residents felt a sense of hope for the first time in their prison careers. Younger residents sought support and advice from staff; the older, more skeptical residents, who felt the effort was an exercise in futility, were more passive. Many residents wondered why they did not get help from staff with some of their "constitutional and committee" questions. Some interpreted it as a sign of resistance; others recognized that many staff were feeling powerless and unhappy because they interpreted the Resident Governmental Council endeavor as divesting them of their power—even though the policy of the Department of Institutions and the laws (RCWs 72.02.040, 72.08.040 and 72.08.045) stated otherwise.[16]

Over time, several "constitutions" were developed in each of the institutions, and the process was in operation. The residents fully recognized that the veto power existed. Stastny and Tyrnauer (*Who Rules the Joint?*) were to report this (later) in their thoughtful sociological study, in which they quoted the Resident Governmental Council as saying that everything Conte had given them supposedly had to be restructured and put through the administration for consent. Thus, the Resident Government Council reported:

> ...even though they took out what they (the administrators) didn't want us to have, the council was able to take credit for what was allowed and then implemented as policy. p.92

I feel the Resident Governmental Council fully recognized its privilege and responsibility when it noted in a revised constitution, also quoted by Stastny and Tyrnauer:

> The Resident Governmental Council will seek through legal and socially acceptable channels to expand the area of its responsibilities...and to implement programs of rehabilitation. The staff was enjoined to carry out its responsibilities accurately and truthfully to the best of their abilities. p.95

These phrases were very encouraging. It was clear that within the newly created program, constructive forces were at work. The need to accept responsibility and to move ahead had been heard and was being acted upon. The call for cooperation and humane treatment was clear. The potential for working together, planning for the future, and finding a ray of hope in what too often had been a pretty dismal world for the resident was within reach. Bob Rhay, always interested in resident education and vocational training, stood strong with his record of accomplishments. Learning in an improved social situation could be rewarding for all. Now, if all parties could find the wisdom and maintain the strength to work together, things could change.

One early change which was brought about by a recommendation of the Resident Governmental Council and endorsed by the administration at Walla Walla was a series of organizations, some for a specific educational purpose and others with a more social orientation. Each had its place. Each provided an opportunity to give the resident a sense of belonging. But each also had its own potential for the quest of power and, in time, many of these organizations added another element in the power struggle between staff, administration and resident.

The power struggle was greatly affected when the creation of DSHS granted unprecedented power to organized labor. As with any community, a prison gets out of hand when one force within it predominates. Under such conditions, the democratic philosophy does not prevail.

7
REORGANIZATION OF STATE GOVERNMENT:
The Department of Social and Health Services

Meanwhile, in the late 1960s, some proposals for administrative change were floating around the State Capitol. The idea was to reorganize state government and reduce the role of the professional in administering programs.

A number of states already had consolidated many of their human or social services into large umbrella agencies. Advocates said such consolidation would increase efficiency and would be cost effective. While that concept was difficult for those of us involved in administering the already-too-large state agencies to embrace, the favorable reports from other states together with the ever present need to save funds gave considerable impetus to consolidation.

It was argued that the statutes requiring the Director of Institutions to hold a doctoral degree was too restrictive. Gradually, but with singular clarity, the word was passed that professionals had a place in program development but that lay administration should run the show.

Looking back and reviewing this change in light of current impressive training programs in public administration, and recognizing the efficiency demonstrated by many of today's program managers, it is clear that these developments in the late '60s were the precursors of modern professional management. However, when viewed from the perspective of that early period, such ideas created considerable anxiety. There were no trained (generic) administrators! Many of the professionals on duty then had acquired superior administrative skills; but those skills had been difficult to develop and were slow in coming. It seemed that capabilities that had been so difficult to attain were about to be scrapped in deference to the creation of positions for which there were no trained personnel.

Specifically, I clearly did not see how the programs could maintain their momentum if professional leadership was to be scuttled. Without strong replacements for that leadership, the faith that new developments would be pursued would be shaken. Without faith, a willingness to cooperate would be in danger.

My greater personal concern related primarily to the corrections field, the last of the areas in the purview of the Department of Institutions to be brought up to date. The task of reform was difficult enough. Finding persons who understood human growth, development and treatment was a most difficult challenge. Finding individuals who could understand and tolerate the behavior of people with character disorders was even harder. Was it possible that the difficult task of bringing about reform was to be complicated by a new dimension: putting less than professionally-trained administrators in charge?

Adding to the anxiety was the fact that whenever the laws pertaining to a particular state-operated program are opened for revision, an opportunity is created for the Legislature and the general public to bring up an unlimited number of proposals for amending it. I do not, of course, oppose the constitutional provision which calls for free speech! But, the moment when one is trying to change the operation of an existing program is not the time to open the entire operation to public discussion and possible revision. Reactionaries with highly personalized motivation involved in such discussions might be sufficiently impressive to bring about legislative action reversing the progress made.

I readily admit my distress was increased when I heard that rumors were being circulated suggesting that "things are out of control in the prisons, residents 'thought' they were in charge," and that some staff feared for their personal safety.

My concerns to the contrary notwithstanding, the Department of Social and Health Services became a reality on January 1, 1971. The pleas for smaller institutions voiced so eloquently by Garrett Heyns had not been heard. In addition to its bigness, which knowledgeable parties knew would be *more*, rather than less, expensive, the new "super agency" had certain built-in problems that foreshadowed disaster. To begin with, the qualifications of the Secretary of DSHS were not spelled out in the statutes, making it easier for appointments to that leadership position to be based on factors other than professional certification. The bill creating the new agency created a director of personnel who would not be under the merit system, leaving open the possibility that appointments would be based on politics rather than qualifications and ability. (This personnel chief would be appointed by the Secretary of DSHS who also was not under the merit system.) Labor-Management disputes could be handled at the central office level between the exempt personnel officer and the Olympia-based union leadership, rather than between superintendents of individual institutions and the local union membership. This laid the groundwork for great difficulty since Olympia is noted for its political pressures from many sources.

Under DSHS, union members actually did not have to do anything they did not want to do. With the organizational structure described above, and with the close proximity of the exempt leadership to the many political pressures in the capitol, job descriptions and requirements could easily be changed to suit the correctional officer, and the on-site program administrator might not have any say.

Prison employees really did not want to change their way of viewing their charges, and they did not want to spend time at the Frye Hotel in Seattle to learn new ways of doing things. Under the new system, they didn't even have to be nice to anyone.

I feared that many simply would not remain in public service under these circumstances — a prediction that turned out to be correct. Many left.

With the passage of the bill creating the Department of Social and Health Services, the union was exuberant, the politicians made speeches about their open door policy toward organized labor, and union leadership responded with great praise for the "insight" of the Legislature.[17] Quite obviously, the power of the union was substantially enhanced and, from my vantage point, Reform was in serious trouble.

Strange, indeed! I had feared that the Black Panthers and Jane Fonda would upset the apple cart by moving too swiftly! In reality, by their vote, the Washington State Legislature had severely threatened, if not destroyed, the administrative structure so essential to the reformation of an archaic prison system. And most of the well-intentioned legislators didn't even know it.

I had urged that correctional services be placed in a separate Department of Corrections since I felt programs to help the welfare mother and the retarded child could not be successfully meshed with the correctional system.

I was given the opportunity to apply for the position of Secretary of the new Department when the search for the "right man" to fill that job was launched. I declined for a number of reasons, not the least of which was the clear recognition that I would not be able to adjust to the new administrative structure which allowed decisions about programs and staff to be made at other than the program level by program people. I mourned for the bygone days of the political insulation so enjoyed during the Heyns era.

It would not be fair to suggest that the several considerations mentioned above were the only problems I saw. The new administration was recruited from the business world which is entirely different from the human services arena. State governmental services for troubled people often don't lend themselves to the same operating principles that apply to business. The motivations and goals are too different for the administrative practices of one to apply directly to the other.

My position is clear: business is dedicated to creating products to be exchanged for dollars. It calls for the management of people, time and equipment. In the human services, the sought-after product is growth in understanding and in interpersonal relationships. Success is dependent upon the nurture of human emotions. Business growth demands speed. Personality growth abhors it.

As it turned out, the administration of the new Department was inexperienced in the field of public service. More importantly, they felt that those who were in state government knew little whereof they spoke. State employees were seen as "feeders at the public trough." Unfortunately, the new leadership in DSHS was not very subtle. It boasted the new Department was going to solve all the problems and do so quickly!

Imagine my surprise when I was approached by an individual serving as an administrative assistant to the new DSHS leadership and told that I would have to "get with it" because everything needed to be changed, and, it would be changed! At the time this dictum was handed to me, I had considerable experience in public programs at all administrative and jurisdictional levels. I had brought the state mental hospitals into the national brotherhood of respectable mental health programs and had spearheaded the changes necessary for the hospitals' full accreditation. In addition, I had opened the doors of the schools for the retarded and brought to them a community orientation. In one legislative session, I had lobbied for and watched 21 different pieces of legislation become law. Now, I was being told to get ready for change!

The man who approached me with this message had not been born at the time I completed my graduate education, and he had no public administrative experience.

It was in this first conference of my "orientation" that I heard two often-to-be-repeated phrases: (a) We do not want corrections to become a political issue, and, (b) We must avoid a riot in Washington at all costs.

Of course, I agreed with the philosophy, but for different reasons.

I was to learn much later that each of the correctional institution superintendents was approached repeatedly in the same vein: get ready for change. Frequently, the representatives of the new administration were from the office of the Attorney General, which had no administrative responsibility or authority in the correctional programs. One warden later told me he was visited weekly over a period of some months and given direct instructions as to what was expected of him. Some of his instructions came via informal opinions from the Attorney General. Another warden was threatened with dismissal if he did not conform to certain dictated patterns of behavior.

DSHS couldn't work, and I knew it. I did not want to be the Assistant Secretary of the Department and preside over the deterioration of that which I had built.

I left the state agency called DSHS on July 1, 1971, excited about what had been demonstrated in the way of prison reform and its potential for turning around the archaic and ineffective prison system, but sad that the political environment was destined to bring these sound developments to an end.

8

WASHINGTON CORRECTIONS VERSUS ATTICA

$\mathbb{C}$alendar year 1971 was perhaps the most exciting period in the Reform Movement. Resident Governmental Councils were hard at work developing their individual constitutions and moving toward a greater degree of cooperation with staff. Involvement of those from within the institution, and interested citizen representatives, signaled a new day in openness for prison management. Although the Resident Governmental Councils were envisioned as only a first step in the democratization of the prison system, they had become instruments of self-government and it was apparent that progress was being made.

Now, if only staff would employ the wisdom to work with those they kept, but had not respected, and if residents could contain their anger long enough to allow productive communications with the powers that be, much could be accomplished.

Wallace Turner, writing in the New York Times on Monday, October 18, 1971, p.24, presented a most comprehensive and objective view of the new look at the Walla Walla institution. I am taking the liberty to extensively quote from his writing.

Turner opens his word picture of the Walla Walla institution by noting:

"Walla Walla, Wash., Oct. 17

A strange prison social structure, perhaps the strangest in the United States, has been formed in the last year at the Washington State Penitentiary.

At the core of the experiment is a representative council of prisoners, elected by the prisoners, who have also written and adopted a constitution. The system seems headed toward the removal of guards from inside the walls and, eventually, to the removal of the walls."

Turner also notes that:

— "Inmates can make telephone calls anywhere...mail is uncensored and a prisoner can send any amount of letters, so long as he pays his own postage."

— "Dress in prison yard is varied."

— "A reporter, alone and unaccompanied by either a guard or a prisoner, is safe to walk through the yard and cell block to talk with inmates who converse easily and openly."

— "There are beards, mustaches, sideburns, and hair in all lengths even though this is a maximum security institution where the 1,155 inmates include the most hardened criminals."

— "A prisoner is no longer punished merely on the word of a guard. Prisoners sit on disciplinary committee meetings. While they do not vote, they discuss the evidence with the correctional staff officers and offer arguments in defense of the prisoners."

— "The inmate government known as the Resident Governmental Council, serves six months...the second elected council was honored at a dinner in the dining hall. About 100 outsiders attended, some of them wives of prisoners, others officials such as the chairman of the Washington Parole Board, others reporters and photographers."

— "(An imate's comments) illustrate one of the fundamental problems of the social structure: How does an inmate politician, elected for a six-month term by his fellow prisoners, maintain his political position while requiring his electorate of lawbreakers to follow some basic rules of behavior? Governor Daniel J. Evans, who has supported the reforms at the prison, said he discussed the problem, a variation of one common to all elected office holders, when he met with members of the convict government in a prison visit a week ago."

— "A civilian advisory committee has been named, as provided in the constitution...the six members were appointed jointly by the prison superintendent and the president of the Resident Government Council...Its (the council's) members include educators, a state employment service officer, a businessman, a lawyer and a psychologist. 'We perceive our role as outsiders seeing what is going on.'"

There is no question but that Prison Reform in Washington averted an Attica-type confrontation. The raw material from which riots are made was certainly present. During the study and planning days of Reform I had seen and felt the more superior-than-thou attitude of the guards, had witnessed the indifference to the needs of the residents of the institutions, and I had heard the deprecatory vocabulary with which the residents had been addressed. Perhaps more than anything else, I had perceived the devastating sense of hopelessness which so permeated the correctional setting.

The Washington Reform effort was in progress for some years before Attica. Many of the problems facing Attica in the fall of 1971 had been solved or substantially alleviated in Washington.

There is a plethora of material on resident complaints registered at Attica and that book need not be written again. Nonetheless, complaints and demands often referred to in reports on Attica are noted here because of their similarity to some once heard and pursued in Washington State.

— The overcrowded population at Attica was composed of individuals who had a history of living with violence in their interpersonal relationships and whose social, moral, and political orientation was entirely foreign to that of their keepers and not understood by them.

— Residents at Attica observed that the average educational level of the guards was a seventh grade education. Men coming to prison in New York had 10 to 11 years of formal schooling, thus "academically we surpass them." (Clark)

— Food was described as deplorable, medical attention inadequate, and there is a need to allow access to outside doctors and dentists.

— There was censorship of residents' mail, newspapers magazines and other publications.

— Residents were addressed in derogatory language, blacks were referred to as "niggers" and "boy" and there was an effort made to keep blacks and whites separated.

— The demand for an improved resident education program including the creation of vocational training for jobs which actually existed outside the walls was a high priority among the residents.

— There was a strong plea made to end the lockup of a resident on the word of a guard and for the creation of a hearing procedure as well as a formal resident grievance procedure.

— Residents asked for adequate shower facilities and permission to use them on a more frequent (than once a week) basis.

— The plea was made to end the practice of physically abusing a resident before he was put in "the box." Residents asked that the practice of guards taking personal possessions of the residents and making the theft appear that another inmate had stolen the property be brought to an end.

— The request was made for prompt consideration of a resident's request for an appointment with a prison official, for legal assistance and a law library, for true religious freedom, protection for residents' funds, and for freedom for political activity among the residents.

— Also among the requests was one for residents to be paid the legal minimum wage for work done to maintain the institution.

A comparison of the complaints registered at Attica without specific program efforts to correct them and those heard earlier in Washington makes it clear that the Washington program had prevented the horror of another Attica.

9

RESISTANCE TO REFORM

It is quite possible that the official launching of resistance to the prison reform movement occurred in September, 1971, when Mr. Sidney Smith, first Secretary of the Department of Social and Health Services paid a surprise visit to the Walla Walla institution. Notes regarding that visit illustrate both the attitudinal and administrative changes that accompanied the creation of DSHS.

Excerpts from those notes, prepared by a resident secretary of the Resident Governmental Council follow:

> From the Rec. Dept., Mr. Smith was then taken to other areas, all the while, Sgt. Moses was stating to Smith, 'I'm for the program, BUT..I believe it will work BUT WE NEED RULES, WE NEED THIS...'The entire evening was spent by Sgt. Moses pointing out the negative side of what has happened, and at every turn, Superintendent Rhay was mentioned in such a way that at one point Mr. Smith remarked: 'Well, MAYBE BOB RHAY HAS BEEN HERE TOO LONG. MAYBE HE NEEDS A CHANGE. MAYBE HE NEEDS TO TAKE THREE MONTHS OFF AND GO SOMEPLACE ELSE.'

After all these jibes which were tossed at Bob Rhay, Mr. Smith said:

> 'Well, THE BUCK STOPS AT ME, AND WHEN I GET BACK TO OLYMPIA, I'LL MAKE THE DECISION ABOUT *SELF*-Government' whether OR NOT WE LET IT CONTINUE OR WHETHER WE SHUT IT DOWN, I'LL MAKE THE DECISION.' Following the conclusion of Mr. Smith's Friday visit, he left, and G. alerted the Maximum R.G.C., and a special all night meeting was held, discussing how we would meet the charges which Sgt. Moses had leveled at population and Bob Rhay...

Mr. Smith began by saying he was no expert on corrections, that he was just becoming acquainted with the problems. He said he would leave the corrections problems to the experts, but he made the point that he didn't want penal reform to become a gubernatorial issue, because there were too many conflicting reports being given as to what was happening here. He went on to state that if penal reform did become a political issue, we will all lose.

Secretary Smith's visit was a monumental event that had far-reaching consequences. When Smith used the term "*self* government," he gave official sanction to the mistaken notion that the program authorized the residents to make their own rules. What had been introduced as a teaching tool had been summarily converted into an administrative one that in fact gave the residents a measure of control. Individuals who had seen this particular reform endeavor as "*self* government" felt confirmed in their belief. The residents of the institutions, always impressed with their powerlessness and deeply involved in a never-ending quest for power, felt strengthened. Correctional staff, on the other hand, already threatened by their charges' new freedom to use the phones, to enjoy work release and furloughs, and the like, could interpret the Secretary's statement as an end to their hope for relief from their fears.

When the Secretary questioned the longevity of the superintendent in his position, he undermined the superintendent's authority. When he said *he* would make the decision about *self* government, he gave notice that the democratic administration of the Department of Institutions was not a philosophy held in high regard by the Department of Social and Health Services. When he said that he was "no expert on corrections," he confirmed what the residents had already come to believe.[18]

And so, resistance to Reform began, best described in its earliest manifestation as "heel dragging." As the advantages handed to organized labor became more apparent, the cleavage between staff and residents became deeper. Staff was upset because there was an extensive proliferation of resident organizations and special interest groups, each with its axe to grind or its philosophy to espouse, and each became increasingly verbal. Minority groups emerged, bearing some proof of the words expressed by the Black Panther representative and giving credence to Jane Fonda's prophecies.

I had always felt that Superintendent Rhay had done an outstanding job in his support of minorities. His introduction of Black study programs into the curriculum of the prisons' training programs was highly commendable. But, I will confess that when I heard of the several "groups" and organizations having their own territory on the prison grounds, and that those areas were off limits to all others, sometimes including staff, I had cause to wonder. I was particularly puzzled since these organizations were in no way a part of our discussions of prison reform.

However, because of the unaltered authority of the superintendents and the knowledge of the availability of their veto power, I rested comfortably, assuming that any loosening of control had, indeed, been accomplished with the approval of the superintendents, whose judgment I trusted, and in whose ability to cope with whatever eventuality might emerge I had confidence.

But in 1974 and 1975, long after I had left state government, I began to hear how out-of-hand the institutions really had become.

In many ways, it seemed as though a paralysis of responsible authority had set in. Guards, acting upon an unfounded idea that the residents were in charge, failed to assume their roles as they pursued a laissez-faire attitude. The superintendents complained that they were accosted by so many managers from DSHS, each proclaiming his authority and handing down new orders, they did not know which way to turn.

When the residents recognized their apparent freedom they responded sometimes defiantly, at other times in open hostility, toward the guards for whom many held so much contempt. There were serious intra-institution abuses, people were hurt, drugs were rampant, etc.

However, even with this understanding, I still have to wonder what happened to the veto power defined as Department Policy when reforms were implemented and so clearly spelled out in the statutes.

Resistance to the Reform Movement was a many-faceted affair. Its presence was felt in such a variety of ways in that, by coincidence, a number of disruptive events took place at the same time.

There were, of course, no secrets. Everyone knew of the changes brought about by the development of the Department of Social and Health Services. They may not have understood all the implications, but they knew Union personnel, the most advantageously affected, were perhaps the best informed. Their newspaper, The Washington State Employee, clearly spelled out the changes.

The changes were quickly and vividly felt in many quarters. The superintendents who were told that, while their previous authority under the Department of Institutions would now be in the hands of the exempt Secretary and exempt personnel chief of DSHS, they need not worry: that authority would be delegated back to them and they would feel no difference in their job or in their ability to carry it out. That authority was never delegated "back" to them.

Instead, the superintendents, traditionally involved in labor-management negotiations at the institution level, felt a sense of isolation created by the transfer of that function to the Olympia arena. They found themselves living with decisions made from afar and made by individuals who did not have knowledge of the corrections field or the practical understanding of the day-to-day institution and administrative problems. Further, they often felt powerless in that many of the decisions they were required to implement had obviously come to the Olympia decision makers via a round-about route and reflected the wishes of union members instead of program persons.

The whole issue of the high level exempt positions in DSHS and the various personnel practices which minimized the role of the Department of Personnel and the merit system unfolded gradually and with a powerful impact. Recognizing the authority held in union hands, it was apparent that union members did not have to perform as required by the Department; instead, they could do what they wished. Generally, what they wanted was a return to the philosophy of "lock them up and don't be bothered by them" endorsed by the "Treat 'em Rough Boys." This was the position their fathers had embraced: just guard them and prevent escapes.

None of this is to imply that the union membership was bent on destroying programs; but clearly union members' needs are more important to them than are the needs of the residents of institutions.

The superintendents perceived keenly the absence of professional leadership in Olympia. Former Superintendent Rhay was to tell me much later that no one could imagine the terrible void he felt after I left Olympia.[19] There was no one to respond on policy or technical matters and no sense of support for the old policies which had emerged in the years of prison reform. Then, confronted with a series of managers who admitted they knew nothing of the field of corrections, but who were proving their authority by "giving orders," the superintendents felt immersed in a world of chaos, and they responded by paralysis. This was added to by a series of Attorney Generals' opinions that had the effect of enforcing the "orders," the inadvisability of so doing notwithstanding.[20]

And, of course, the resident, happy with the advantages offered by prison reform, and faced with the new administration which wanted to be sure prisons did not become a political topic, were equally confused. On the one hand they were encouraged to rebel by certain resident activists and confronted by the guards who felt that he no longer even had to speak to a resident if he didn't want to. The conflicts were ready-made and waiting for expression.

Clearly, the enabling act bringing about the Department of Social and Health Services had destroyed the balance of power so essential to smooth working and learning relationships. My predictions about the effect of DSHS had been proven correct.

10
NATURE OF INSTITUTIONS

This thesis requires further elucidation of the character of institutions.

Institutions, whether public or private, are small communities or, sometimes, large ones. They are composed of housing facilities, food services, schools and training programs, and laws. They are, of course, created to serve people who, whether voluntary citizens or involuntarily committed individuals, carry with them certain basic rights, needs and ambitions. As in all communities, institution residents tend to band together to improve their environment and voice their hopes and to seek redress for their complaints. From such groupings there emerge leaders who promise to satisfy these personal hopes.

If this description of a community within an institution sounds familiar to the reader who hopes the city council will enforce zoning requirements, or that the state senator will work to avoid tax increases, then my point has been made.

There are, however, two striking differences between the ordinary community and the corrections community. The residents of the corrections community are there because they need to learn better ways of relating to others; and, the superintendent of the institution is charged with the responsibility of seeing that the "better ways" are taught.

From time immemorial, correctional superintendents have governed with the use of resident (inmate) help. Before Reform, that help was secretive and based on "tough guy" intimidation and violence. This approach could scarcely be viewed as rehabilitative. Instead, it provided an arena for abuse of residents, which at times engendered anger that knew no limits. Reform was an effort to rehabilitate residents in part by requiring a nonviolent, democratic, participatory approach to helping residents. The Resident Governmental Council, acting under the supervision of the superintendent, was the teaching tool to convey the fundamentals of community participation to those who seemed not to have learned it before they came to prison.

It is an axiom of human behavior that the governed are peacefully governable when there is a willingness to be governed. That willingness to be governed emerges when the individual views himself as a member of the group and when he understands the advantages of cooperative co-existence. Such conditions, and a sense of personal respect, create the desire and strongly support the individual's participation in the process of government. Every law-abiding citizen realizes this; unfortunately, it is a concept that has escaped the attention of many convicted felons.

Those who govern are successful when they perceive the needs and problems of those they govern. A successful governor — of a state, a family, a prison — is able to rate his efforts on how well the governed actually do, what progress they make, and what they learn. A successful governor also will look with pride on how he has enhanced the human condition.

Prisons are unique communities. Their citizens are troubled, and they have been in trouble. The nature of the clientele makes prisons the ultimate challenge of the governors. They are further unique in that the special kinds of human problems in prisons require of their governors a degree of expertise in the field of human behavior.

Our efforts in the '50s and '60s were predicated on the premise that that sophistication could be taught to larger and larger segments of the staff. Thus, the Philosophy of Corrections, the on-site experiences in the ghetto, the in-service training programs, and on and on, held high the objective of helping staff learn more and more about whom they served.

Prisons have always had a varied quality of administrative and resident leadership. Motivational factors and personality have seemed to identify the leaders within prison groups. Wardens have been appointed by their central administrations. Both sides have served their masters, sometimes well and sometimes not so well. Competitions have been great. Wardens have ofttimes used resident leadership to separate themselves from resident needs and demands or to enhance their positions. Often they have had to rely on rigidity and force to maintain peace. Resident leadership has been more effective where diplomacy has been employed. Underhanded exploitation of either side has generally ended in chaos.

The community called a prison, its admixture of troubled citizens and the imposition of a wide variety of administrative motivations and techniques, and its tradition of inattention to people needs was the raw material upon which prison reform was based.

Given an inherent resistance to change and the special problems faced in prison reform, together with the unique difficulties encountered in the prison community, the authority called for in the total responsibility mandated in the 1960s had to be strong and undivided. The Department of Social and Health Services weakened that authority and disrupted the balance of power so necessary in the governance of any community.

11
AND LATER

Although I left state government in 1971, I kept abreast of the many developments through personal relationships formed over the twelve years of my involvement in the state's institutional programming (1959-1971). Further, the press seemed always eager to get my view on various issues and each such contact helped keep my information current. Then, too, there was a steady flow of residents from the correctional facilities, either on work release or parole, who kept in touch or visited me in my private office. So I stayed aware of what was going on behind the walls.

Administrators in the field felt isolated from their central administration and powerless given the new labor-management relationships created by DSHS. No prison reform was announced as such or implemented after I left office. Without the hope of further progress, the residents of institutions became discouraged and bitter. Both the guards and the residents focused on the past. For the residents, the past was without hope. For the correctional officers, the past was more comfortable; it was a time when they were required only to enforce the rules. Regression to that earlier way of thinking and doing came easy. As time passed and the residents became increasingly aware that their hope for decent treatment was disappearing, they grew more upset and testy.

The emerging clash between residents and staff was only one of the wounds that began to ooze the venom of disrespect each faction showed the other. In addition to groups formed for socializing, several organizations and clubs that had emerged in the Walla Walla institution and that had been endorsed by the administration became powerful lobbying forces within the institutions during the early 1970s. There were the bikers, the Black Panthers, and other groups representing segments of the Black Power movement of the day. Many of these organizations, and the individuals who joined them, were strenuously fighting their own broad social battles which had emerged from two hundred years of neglect and prejudice, both inside and outside the institutions. There was much to be said for their outlook since there was then, and still is, a large discrepancy in the number of minorities as opposed to whites represented in prison populations.

The old line staff who saw this population as nothing but "animal" in the first place, didn't receive well the angry voices raised against them. Certainly these groups "should not be allowed" to express themselves so freely while they were being "cared for" in a state correctional institution, it was argued.

In the troubled days after the resistance to Reform "set in," there seemed to be a steady supply of drugs and alcohol coming into the prisons. While there is much evidence that the delivery of contraband was made by family members or friends, it would seem that by the mid '70s there was a more dependable supply from some place. It has been suggested that it arrived with the help of some who came to the institution daily and who might have used the illegal substances as tools or bribes in regaining control over a then more independently-thinking population.

Some called for an investigation on how drugs were being slipped into the prisons. I could, of course, understand their concern: smuggling cannot be condoned anyplace. But, when I heard of the uproar over marijuana, I could not help but think of the resistance that would have come about if I had had the opportunity to introduce conjugal visits, my next goal had I remained part of the program. I could almost hear certain voices suggesting that having sex for the prisoner "might be harmful to his health."

Political maneuverings among residents were legion. Select prisoners who had been favored by the prison leadership had been the government of the prison in its traditional past. Under Reform, they had to surrender their power to a democratic approach, and they wanted it back. A dethroned monarch is never a contented one!

I have always felt that being the only reform endeavor in the nation at the time created many hardships for the Washington program. The programs were given publicity in national news journals and were studied by sociologists and psychologists in depth. Two books have emerged from the undertaking. The national attention given to the work and resistance to it gave each of the factions involved a substantial audience. But those of us involved in Reform really had no current kindred reformers with whom to identify.

Perhaps the saddest of all the opposing groups were the families of the staff. These good people feared for the lives of their loved ones, the guards, as prison unrest mounted. The guards themselves were quoted in the press as sensing that a stigma was associated with their employment. One was quoted as saying, "It goes with the job, for Walla Walla is a small college town. On the campuses, guards are often viewed as lower class, poorly educated people who are only a notch above the inmates they patrol...Even garbage men and mail men get an occasional Christmas card from clients, thanking them, but the prison guard accepts a completely thankless job." (Spokesman Review, 11/20/77)

How unfortunate! These were the very people on whom reform in prisons depended. They were the ones who were targeted for the training programs, who had been called on to be understanding in personal contacts with troubled residents. They had missed their chance...for this time, anyway.

The superintendents, like the rest of us, are only human. They had joined with the more liberal governor and me to bring about change. They were, obviously, much appreciated by the residents of their respective institutions and often resented by staff. When the superintendents were criticized by the union leadership or the media, they were often defended by the residents, who had come to see the administration as trying to be helpful in their troubled lives.

When Secretary Smith made his now-famous first trip to Walla Walla, the Resident Governmental Council stayed up all night preparing to defend their superintendent, who had been criticized by his own staff. Much later, when a walk away from the state penitentiary committed a murder, (an ever-present threat in the release of any person), the Resident Governmental Council made it clear that they supported the superintendent.

It must be remembered that the institutions (that is, Monroe and Walla Walla) were somewhat isolated from the mainstream. I often felt these superintendents must be lonely without the opportunity to talk to people who would understand their responsibilities and the goal of their efforts.

When neither faction in the institutions could be satisfied, the superintendents did, indeed, stand alone.

Being human they, like everyone else, must have had their breaking points!

Superintendent Rhay was accused of not trying.[21] It must now be clear that he did not use the veto power vested in him by the Legislature and the Department to the extent he might have used it. It was published that he said he "would give Conte enough rope and allow him (Conte) to hang himself." His statement suggests he could no longer carry on against the pressures he felt. Could the superintendents have given up, become discouraged and become unable to maintain their stand, given the absence of support from Olympia?

The answers to many questions will probably never be known. What *is* known, however, is that with the passage of time and the recognition of the altered power structure (after DSHS) within the communities called prisons, conflicts broke out at many levels. The residents had had a taste of decent care and they did not want to lose it. The guards wanted a return of their power to control, the basic premise of the treatment program calling for a different orientation notwithstanding. Attica in the State of Washington had been postponed, to be sure. And if Reform had been allowed to continue as planned, all parties could have continued to live and learn together. Instead, chaos was destined to occur.

Charles Stastny and Gabrielle Tyrnauer, researchers at Harvard University's Center for European Studies, brought their sociological and anthropological talents together in their book, *Who Rules the Joint?*, a study of the *Changing Political Culture of Maximum-Security Prisons in America*, (Lexington Books, 1982). In this writing they deal extensively with the "aftermath of reform at Walla Walla." Their material is comprehensive and has already been referred to above. In addition, I have relied heavily on their work in the remaining paragraphs of this portion of my writing. The quotes in this section are all from their text.

The September, 1971 visit of the Secretary Smith revealed a tension between staff and Superintendent Rhay. Some saw his support of Reform as a disloyalty to them. Quite obviously, union membership was already feeling its strength when it could so openly bad-mouth the Superintendent.

At the same time, residents were sensing the loss of the opportunities for growth that had been afforded them under the Reform Movement. While they were confused by what some saw as the Superintendent's tendency to "divide and conquer," they were also sympathetic toward him and supportive when unfortunate incidents occurred.[22]

Their sympathetic attitude toward the Superintendent notwithstanding, some residents saw the developing conflict between the guards and the institution leadership as an opportunity to espouse their causes more forcefully. These forces tended to play the conflict for their own selfish gains. Attempts were made to get staff and residents working together, with the staff being encouraged in a new Resident Governmental Council constitution, to carry out its responsibilities "accurately and truthfully...to the best of (our) abilities."

Many sensed the pleasure of the union with the various manifestations of prison disorganization. Stastny quoted a union president as saying "The prison regime has grown so loose this doesn't even look like a penitentiary." Unfortunately, it must not have looked like an institution for learning a new lifestyle, either!

After much stress and many failed efforts to enhance communications, Superintendent Rhay announced on April 2, 1975, that the Resident Governmental Council had been dissolved. A new council was established, but it had little if any effect on improving the relationship between residents, staff, and the administration.

Among the problems in the institutions in the mid 1970s were the several special interest groups, each espousing its own cause and maintaining its exclusivity. Each limited its memberships to only a chosen few. This type of activity was not in any way related to prison reform; in fact, it ran counter to the democratic principles that Reform was designed to teach. The various groups became caught up in territorial struggles over control of a few square feet of ground within the prison walls or an unused room or shack they considered to be "theirs." (See *The Concrete Mama.*)

In time, the Resident Governmental Council and other groups, had become politicized, with the various members serving their own needs rather than the needs of those they represented.

A number of committees were appointed to study the prison unrest, and the Institutions Committee of the House of Representatives called a hearing. Grievances of the residents were aired; they were not unlike those heard in the past. High level prison administrators concluded that some of their grievances were justified, but they pronounced overcrowding to be the problem.

As the years went by, the Walla Walla institution saw the perpetuation of the clash between the traditional prison philosophy and the stalwarts of Reform, who still recognized an obligation to implement the rehabilitative approach ordained by the Legislature. Superintendents had to deal with angry residents as well as guards who saw no advantage in the changes. Security was tightened, efforts were made to curtail the passage of drugs through the gates, riots ensued and hostages were taken. Violence persisted. The time and attention of the institution leadership were hopelessly divided between conflicting parties, resulting in a horrendous loss of energy and dollars.

On July 7, 1979, guard brutality reached its highest peak of immorality when a resident of the institution was raped with a night stick (See Appendix). The American Civil Liberties Union filed for "injunctive relief against overcrowding and guard brutality, for damages for beatings, and for damages for loss of personal property." The federal judge hearing the case issued the injunction while the Secretary of DSHS defended the guards. But a medical report confirmed the night stick rape and it was abundantly clear that the brutality had occurred.

A special master appointed by the federal court held hearings and concluded special efforts were needed to deal with racial violence within the prison. "...other witnesses decried the state's abominable plan for the guards' racial sensitivity training as inadequate and deplored the widespread belief among guards that prisoners (especially minorities) are less than fully human." (Stastny and Tyrnauer, *Who Rules the Joint?*, p.113, quoting The Seattle Post-Intelligencer on Dec. 6, 1980.) The course had run full cycle. The guards, in spite of extensive training in the Reform Movement, had not really changed. Perhaps they even had regressed. They still viewed their charges as animals.

12
IN CONCLUSION

I could not compose a scenario with as many intrigues, varying motivations, mixed reactions and influences as the one which emerged as the correctional Reform Movement of the '50s and '60s moved into the 1970s. What follows is my view of how the various factions saw the situation.

The View From the Executive Office: There could never be two governors who more genuinely hoped for and worked for an improvement in the care of residents of state-operated institutions. Governor Daniel J. Evans, who was to become more involved in prison reform than Governor Rosellini, was always supportive and frequently inserted in his public utterances strong arguments in favor of reform. Although the DSHS was developed in response to an executive request, I know the Governor had no thought this umbrella agency, anticipated as an administrative advancement for state government, would have created such difficulties in the management of individual programs. (See Appendix: Bogan, in *The Spokesman Review*.) The Governor and his staff were stunned by the resistance the Resident Governmental Council evoked and, at times, they could not believe that such negative attitudes were at play. They argued no one could oppose teaching residents new and better roles for citizen participation.

From the Vantage Point of the Staff (The Guards): The changes expected of them seemed impossible for them to understand. They were being asked to assume a new, communicative approach to a segment of the population who had behaved in unsavory ways. That new approach was entirely different from the one they had always utilized. I believe the training programs for staff at all levels were excellent and I know that many learned new and appropriate ways of relating; but, was it enough? Could it have been taught differently?

127

What could have been done to have helped the trainees put their training to better use? Or, was the material to be taught too much of a change for the traditionalists to ever comprehend, let alone accept? While no answers to these questions are possible, one thing can be said for certain: when DSHS provided fertile ground for their resistance to flourish, they exploited that opportunity, even though their failure to move ahead with the Reform program was clearly not in their own best interest. To support the downfall of Reform was to invite the continuation of failure with which their past was shrouded.

In fairness, it should be noted that mixed messages coming with the passage of time must have created a very confusing situation for the guards. They knew of, and many had seen, the reforms implemented over many years, and some strongly supported them. But when local institution leadership felt stranded and appeared to drag its heels or failed to adequately support the Resident Governmental Council, many were confused. Many must have wondered, "What is really expected of me?" Faced with such a confused picture, they understandably followed their union leadership, and relied on their statewide organization's gains in DSHS to resist the change.

The institution superintendents and their leadership team continue to receive my sympathy and understanding. Theirs was a most difficult position. Most had gone through the tedious discussions about improvement in the corrections programs, had cooperated with architects about structures, had consulted with trainers on the teaching programs, had attended meeting after meeting to plan new approaches to the old problems. All this they had done in good spirit and with enthusiasm. Freeman had expressed it well in 1952 when he noted it was time to change. And change they did.

But, after DSHS came into being, they no longer were the managers of their own institutions, and no longer could they even be assured that their position would be heard when labor negotiations took place.

With DSHS, managers from the business community had taken over. Administrative policies and approaches were dictated from above. The democratic approach to administration, to which the superintendents had been accustomed under the Department of Institutions' Philosophy of Administration, was lost. Now, if superintendents procrastinated for a moment, they were confronted the next day with "an order" from the office of the Attorney General, or so they perceived it.

I think the superintendents did not know what to do. Caught between good programs to enhance the human condition of the residents and the resistance from staff, and burdened by a hurry-up undemocratic attitude on the part of new DSHS bosses eager to demonstrate the "success" of the super agency, they fell into a general state of frustration, depression and paralysis.

I have noted that the Veto Power was not used when it should have been exercised. I cannot resent that inactivity in the light of the environment in which the superintendents found themselves.

From my perspective I observed that professionalism was no longer respected; instead, it was replaced by those that didn't cost as much. The Philosophy of Administration, an unheard-of dictum before the Heyns-Conte era, was totally ignored as people were told what they would do and how they would do it. Communications between staff, the superintendents, and my office, which had been so difficult to establish and so diligently pursued, deteriorated day by day as a result of the administrative chaos.

Some were to say that the Four Reforms of November, 1970, were precipitously ordained without adequate preparation. I think the preparation for the Reform had been adequate. Twenty years of Reform Movement should have communicated clearly that change was occurring. The crux of the matter is that Reform got started and was clearly destined to be interrupted. Had we waited longer, the Four Specific Reforms would not have been introduced or tried at all. Those ideas would have simply been filed away along with other ideas from the past which never had a chance to succeed.

From the view of the residents of the correctional programs there was confusion, followed by anger. They profited from the Reform Movement. Many were getting GEDs, diplomas from local schools, training in various skills, and they were receiving good counseling services. They showed a spirit of cooperation as they were offered the opportunity to express their views in a representative forum. When these potential avenues for growth were curtailed, they were angered.

A wonderful opportunity to enhance the state services for residents of the correctional institutions and for the protection of The Public was put on hold while factions fought. But the programs were not lost. Eventually they got back on course in one form or another. I am convinced from recent visits with those currently in charge that the Reform Movement is in the late '80s moving on.

The Reform Movement of the '50s and '60s clearly had its successes. The physical facilities are greatly improved, as is food service and medical attention. Work-and-training release programs are utilized effectively at Walla Walla and Monroe, though not as extensively at Purdy and Shelton, which institutions were built close to metropolitan centers in order to ensure that advantage. Mail censorship hasn't returned and the right to make collect phone calls continues to allow residents an opportunity to maintain contact with family. The strip cell is not used. And resident participation in each institution is vastly improved over what existed prior to the Reform Movement, with the programs at the Monroe Reformatory most nearly resembling the concept of the Resident Governmental Council created long ago.

Any indication of resident abuse today is quickly and summarily dealt with.

The future will require more reforms in prisons. The preservation of our society demands we get serious about trying to change criminal behavior. When that time comes, I hope the leaders of the day will recall the efforts made by so many in the '50s and '60s.

Our efforts in Reform ran parallel to those of others who embraced the same goals. J.E. Baker, in his historically significant volume entitled, *The Right to Participate: Inmate Involvement in Prison Administration*, (Scarecrow Press, 1974), describes a commonality of philosophies and experience among prison reformers. Baker notes,

> ...Through two centuries of neglect, the prison has functioned apart from the social mainstream, largely ignored, and fulfilling neither the purpose for which it was established nor the dreams of the handful of dedicated men and women who dared step off the treadmill of tradition.

> ...Society and...prison management...must define the role of the prison, say what it is and say what it is not...It has been said...an objective is to assist the individual prisoner to acquire modes of coping...which do not result in conflict with authority. p.243

I feel that in Washington the mandate was clearly described in the statutes which call for rehabilitation along with protection of the public. Until such time as that language is removed from the law, there is no question that treatment efforts must be given highest priority in budget development and manpower distribution. Baker continues,

> ...Every person in a correctional confinement facility should be assured of the right to participate in matters relating to his personal welfare by contributing his point of view.

Correctional leadership has the obligation to make the satisfaction of that right a reality. There is no logical place for resistance to resident participation on his own behalf.

In referring to advisory councils as an opportunity for treatment, Baker calls attention to the opportunity they offer for affecting the attitudinal changes through which more satisfactory modes of coping with social role demands can be realized. p.243

I would hope that everything that happens to the resident while he is in prison would have a therapeutic advantage for him.

In quoting from the *Manual of Correctional Standards (1959)*, Baker notes,

> ...inmate participation in planning and operation of institutional programs is slowly passing out of the controversial stage, and...many prison administrators recognize the approach and method as being sound in educational theory and practical as a means of prison administration. p.244

> Of all the techniques for changing behavior, the impact of one human being on another is probably the most effective. This imposes a tremendous responsibility on the correctional worker, since the direction of that change may rest in the hands of the worker. p.248

Job descriptions should reflect the expectation that treatment (rehabilitation) is the goal of incarceration.

Baker concludes,

> Decisions should be made by those who must justify their choices and be held accountable for the results. p.252

A prerequisite to the making of decisions is a fund of knowledge about the nature of human behavior. Additionally, decision makers in state-operated facilities must have freedom to move within a structure of support provided from the highest level in state government.

Carl Harp.

No account of prison reform in Washington which I might write would be complete without a few comments about Carl Harp. The story of his later days is well documented by Bogan in the *Spokesman-Review* articles. (See Appendix) But, there was an earlier chapter about which Bogan was unaware.

Soon after I became Director of Institutions and had assumed the role of prison reformer, Carl Harp went AWOL from one of the correctional facilities. He was a criminal with a bad history. His behavior was bad and destined to get worse. He was everything undesirable and typified what in today's world would be viewed as "useless, not worth bothering with," someone we should just "lock up and forget."

But Carl was a perceptive individual in his rather primitive way, and he had deep feelings. He was also poorly managed, but he read the reform writings well and he perceived the goal of Prison Reform.

While on his unofficial leave from corrections, Carl called me and we had an in depth conversation. He wanted to turn himself in because he knew that was required by law. He was afraid he would face retaliation for his escape because he had witnessed what happened to others in the same situation. He expressed himself freely, and I responded in like kind — directly, honestly, and to the point. Ultimately, we came to the point where he asked for my recommendation. I spoke clearly on the side of the law and in terms of what was right: he should give himself up. There were no strings attached in our conversation. He did know that I would appear before the Parole Board when he was called and that I would tell everything I knew about him including the fact that he had agonized over "right and wrong" and had decided of his own free will to return, albeit that decision was made with my encouragement.

On his way back to Seattle to surrender to authorities, he was picked up by the police, who enjoyed bold headlines about their capture of this dangerous man. I suspected that no one, save Carl and me, knew he was telling the truth when he stated he was "coming back." I did, of course, keep my word and testified as to my experience with him. The rest of his story has been covered by Bogan.

The experience taught lessons to two people: one, a convict, hardened in the ways of the street, who discovered that he had it within his power to do what was expected of him. The other person involved, an administrator, with hope for a better future for those who were caught up in the system, sensed again that support and sound reasoning, without hostility, could be utilized to reach the most recalcitrant.

My faith that correctional programming could become an effective method of dealing with one of our greater social problems was affirmed by our contact. I had seen it again in operation.

I join Carl in his sense of sadness as I read the following excerpt from a Bogan article on November 21, 1979, under the title of *Fury in the Soul: Inmate's View*

Carl Harp is a good example of an inmate who has elevated inmate pride and dignity to the level of near revolutionary doctrine. After this summer's riots at the prison, Harp, who charged he was beaten and raped with a nightstick by guards, was transferred from Walla Walla to California's San Quentin Prison.

In a personal journal written two weeks after he was transferred, Harp gave a plaintive voice to his outrage at the way he and others have been treated inside the walls.

"Everything is so sad," he wrote, "and I feel so tired of it all but I will not give up the struggle, even if it kills me. I am a man, a human being, and I have the right to be free of this injustice, this inhumanity, to me and around me. Give me strength, give me courage, for I am so weak and scared in here, so alone in reality even with what friends I have." Harp still signs his letters to friends in Washington with the parting salutation: "Love and Rage."

An Informal Consultation.

On one of my many visits to the Washington State Penitentiary in Walla Walla, I chanced to come upon an ancient resident of the institution who was basking in the sun while sitting on a bench outside the main dining room. I asked if I might join him and chat. Poor fellow — he was flustered by my inquiry. I immediately sensed he knew who I was and that he was unaccustomed to having anyone ask for permission to address him. I rather quickly learned that he had been in the institution for many years and was a member of the Lifers' Club. I asked if he anticipated leaving the institution, and he replied that he hoped not. He had been incarcerated too long and felt sure he could not manage outside. (I later learned he had been committed for murder.)

In our conversation, which must have gone on for twenty minutes or so, I asked how he felt about the changes he had seen in the prisons. He felt positively about them, mentioning particularly that the opportunity to use the telephones was wonderful. He had one living relative, a sister, who lived halfway across the country and he had not talked to her for years. This would be his only chance to talk with her since she was too pressed for money to travel to Walla Walla for a visit.

But, as for other anticipated changes, he was not so sure. He expressed great reservations about the "self-government" idea. He felt it could not work.

There followed a sociological dissertation in which he clearly stated that the structure inside the walls would not permit change. As he viewed the situation, the "guards" liked it the way it was. They had not had to give thought to anything except the rules. The "inmate" cops "ran the joint" and the superintendent merely managed the budget and dealt with the visitors from Olympia. No one wanted to talk to prisoners and no one wanted to give up his role. He was particularly firm that he personally did not want to see any more changes. When I asked why he did not welcome a voice in expressing his demands to the administration, he replied, "I don't have any demands." He also revealed that everyone left the old people alone, and that was the way he wanted it.

As I listened, I became aware I was listening to a man whose spirit had been broken and whose depression had become a way of life. His individuality had been ignored for such a long time he could no longer identify it. As we finished our conversation, he thanked me for speaking to him and wished me well in what we were trying to accomplish in the prison system.

In spite of his calm manner, the old gentleman's words of wisdom were firmly imprinted on my thinking. As I left Walla Walla the next day I was troubled. The slow but certain destruction of the humanness of the individual had clearly been demonstrated to me in the old man with whom I had visited. His years of incarceration in the traditional public-supported prison had deprived him of his will. There were many before him who had been destroyed and, unhappily, there would be many more to come. The cycle had not yet been interrupted.

Could there be any question as to why prison reform was (is) so important and necessary?

FINI

A number of things about the reform efforts have sustained me and continue to give me a sense of pride and satisfaction as I look back almost twenty years after my departure from Washington State service. I quote them here because I enjoy rethinking them:

— After I appeared before the Parole Board in the spring of 1971 to tell them that Carl Harp had cooperated with me as I had encouraged him to obey the law and turn himself in, Harp arose to shake my hand and said, "Thank you, you tried to help me." I sensed that he spoke for many.

— Milton Burdman, former Associate Director of Corrections after my departure from state government, addressing the District Branch of the American Psychiatric Association, referred to our efforts when he said, "What Dr. Conte did was wonderful, and it was terrible. He dared to suggest that people with bad behavior were human beings and they could be dealt with. The world was not ready for this concept."

— At my last meeting with then Governor Daniel J. Evans, after I had declared my intention to leave his cabinet, the Governor commented that he had learned of and felt the resistance encountered in the reform movement. He suggested that individuals are inclined to become very conservative when one tries to make changes. Nonetheless, he was certain the message had been heard.

— At the time this book goes to press, it appears that all of the structual reforms instituted in the fifties and sixties have been preserved or reestablished, with modifications to meet changing times and changing budgets. The emphasis, of course, has, in many instances, undergone a rather remarkable metamorphasis.

READING NOTES

(1)   This is Principle II adopted by the National Conference on Penitentiary and Reformatory Discipline (1870), from Transactions of the Congress on Penitentiary and Reformatory Discipline, published by The American Corrections Association, 1970, p.548.

(2)   Selected Writings of Garrett Heyns, William R. Conte, Editor, p.111.

(3)   Perspective, Vol. 13, No. 2, p.26

(4)   RCW 72.08.101 calls for treatment of prisoners in corrective, rehabilitative and reformative programs and procedures for convicted persons at the state penitentiary, which are designed to be corrective, rehabilitative and reformative of the undesirable behavior problems of such persons, as distinguished from programs and procedures essentially penal in nature. (1965)

    The 1979 amendments to the bill left this section unchanged.

(5)   In the *Transactions of the National Congress on Penitentiary and Reformatory Discipline* [field of study] held in Cincinnati, Ohio, October 12-18, 1870, and published by the American Correctional Association one hundred years later, is to be found the paper by Rev. James Woodworth, Secretary of the California Prison Commission. He noted it was only in recent times that it was considered important to provide special training for those who would be teachers of the "common schools. Earlier," he said, the "teacher of this class of schools was...a broken-down merchant, a clerk whom nobody wanted, a consumptive or other person physically incapable of manual labor" — anybody, in short, who had shown himself an imbecile at all other employments, if he had possessed himself of a smattering of the three Rs — "reading, writin' and 'rithmetic." He correlated that position to one held at the time in regard to the qualifications of the person working in a prison. "Any man of fair sense, tolerable education, moderate

executive ability, a dash of energy, and possessing a vigorous frame and sinewy arm, is deemed qualified to take the place even of the head of a prison, though he may never have been inside of penitentiary walls or given the subject of penitentiary discipline a solitary thought." In noting that European correctional systems were ahead of those in America, he commented:

> When Demetz, more than 30 years ago, was about to open the reformatory-agricultural colony of Mettray, in France, which has since made him famous, what most troubled him, in the anticipation, was the problem of how to obtain fit assistants to help him in his work. He felt profoundly that the success of the enterprise depended upon their adequate preparation for the great work to be committed to them...Mr. Demetz...found the true solution when they [he and his colleague] resolved, instead of building high and massive walls for the restraint of their future wards, to educate the guardians who were to control and train them, thus substituting...moral for material forces. [Thus, instead of opening their establishment at once, they and their chaplains spent the first six months in a laborious training of their helpers...Their course of instruction embraced religion, the French language, arithmetic, linear drawing, geography, natural history, geometry...[with] special lessons on the nature, objects, and processes of the great work at hand — that of changing bad boys into good ones.

(6)   See Conte, William R. and Demeter, Katherine. Electroencephalograms Correlated with Commitment Data on 270 Offenders. Clinical Electroencephalography, 1976. Vol. 7, #1.

(7)   From, Delinquency and Crime. An Overview of Theories of Causation. Bulletin, Department of Institutions, April 1970. This article was used extensively in the teaching program associated with the Reform Movement.

(8)   Mr. Freeman's conclusions were entirely accurate when he expressed them in 1957. Unfortunately they reveal the lack of progress made by the correctional discipline over time. See transactions of the Congress on Penitentiary and Reformatory Discipline, Principle III, p.548 and p.i, this writing.

(9)   The announcement in Perspective, August 1957, p.1: A veteran Michigan penologist, Dr. Garrett Heyns, was named by Governor Albert D. Rosellini August 3rd, [1957] to become Director of the Department of Institutions, taking over the office which Dr. G. Lee Sandritter has held in an acting capacity for the past year. Dr. Heyns, 66, with a background of 20 years experience with Michigan penal institutions, leaves the position he held since 1949 as warden of the Michigan State Reformatory at Ionia to accept the directorship of the Depart-

ment at Olympia sometime this month. This appointment will mark the third time a penologist has assumed the state's top administrative office for institutions since January 1954, when Fred R. Dixon was borrowed from the California Department of Corrections to fill the post of Superintendent of Institutions within the newly reorganized Department of Public Institutions...(Dixon was succeeded by Dr. Clarence Schrag...who served in an acting capacity until the appointment of Dr. Thomas A. Harris, a psychiatrist, in June 1955.)

(10)   Director Heyns was dedicated to the concept of smaller institutions. Nonetheless, he encouraged study of alternative methods of service delivery to the wide range of individuals (and disabilities) which came to rest as responsibilities of the Department of Institutions. Thus, in 1961-62, he was strongly supportive of the Department's study of amalgamating the services of the Department of Institutions with other state agencies such as the Department of Health and the Department of Welfare. That undertaking was under the leadership of John W. Baker, social work supervisor in the Division of Mental Health. Mr. Baker's plan was given careful scrutiny and abandoned on the basis that a large umbrella agency would be both inefficient and unreasonably expensive.

The possibility of community based centers to deal with problems of mental health, retardation, and corrections was investigated fully but also abandoned when the families of the retarded made it clear they would not want retarded individuals working in close proximity with individuals having other human problems.

See: The Conte Papers, Washington Room, Washington State Library, Master files M 303 and M 319.

(11)   I was fortunate to have been an early day participant in the new Director's study and his program development. My communications with him were frequent, open and always of the highest quality. He had the ability to inspire and to motivate others. He recognized the feelings and attitudes of others and utilized his perceptions in working with people to accomplish goals. Viewing him in action from my professional orientation in psychiatry was at times a surprise and always a delight.

Heyns saw Washington citizens as socially-minded individuals who wanted to improve services to those who came under the jurisdiction of the Department of Institutions. He encouraged staff to cultivate the public's interest and participation. "An involved public is the key to successful program development," was his often heard admonishment.

Heyns was later to tell me that ours was an unusual opportunity. Perhaps never again would two public administrators have such an opportunity to move services ahead. The people were listening, the Legislature was intrigued, and the Governor was stick ing to his word and was strongly supportive. With planning and deliberate steps forward, Washington's programs for its people could be the best anywhere, but such leadership required much energy and the constant pursuit of quality.

(12)   With the encouragement of Garrett Heyns, personnel from the Department of Institutions became involved in the following organizations and committees:

American Correctional Association

Correctional Administrators Association

American Social Health Association

American Psychiatric Association

Association of Juvenile Compact Administrators

Children's Center, University of Washington

State Civil Defense

Community Planning Advisory Board

Council for Children and Youth

Advisory Board to the Secretary of H.E.W. and the United States Attorney General on Programs for Vocational Training of Adult Offenders

American Association for Mental Deficiency

Council of State Governments, Committee on Juvenile Delinquency

Donations and Contributions Committee

Governor's Advisory Council on Aging Governor's Medical Advisory Committee American Association for Occupational Therapy

National Council on Social Welfare

Governor's Inter Agency Committee on Health, Education, Welfare, and Public Assistance

Subcommittees of Inter Agency Committee:

Alcoholism

Mental Health

Migrant Farm Program

Research Committee

Retardation

White House Conference

Legislation Medical Services Committee

Health Department:

Committee on Coordination of Chronic Illness

Washington State Hospital and Medical Facilities Advisory
Council

Boarding Home Task Force

Interfaith Advisory Committee

Institutional Industries Commission

Joint Commission on Correctional Manpower and Training

Inter Departmental Committee on Delinquency Control

Manpower Training Commission

National Council on Crime and Delinquency

National Council on State Committees for Children and Youth

President's Committee on Law Enforcement and Administration of Justice

Sexual Psychopath Advisory Commission

Governor's Safety Committee

United Good Neighbors

Washington State Councils and Committees:

Emergency Medical Services

State Hospital and Medical Facilities Advisory Committee

State Nurses Association

Corrections Association

Western Interstate Commission on Higher Education in:

Juvenile Delinquency

Research

Training and Research

Staff Development

Equal Employment Opportunities

Title II (Department of Public Instruction) Advisory Committee

Title XI (Public Assistance) Task Force

School of Social Work, University of Washington.

(13)   Statistical evaluation of a public service agency and its functions is always difficult given the multiplicity of methods used to collect the basic information. Recidivism rates, perhaps one of the more significant statistical method of reporting on prison performance is particularly confusing since rates for individuals who return to prison in one year versus five or ten years are markedly different. Nonetheless, according to the Washington State Department of Corrections, the Recidivism Study Preview, 1978, the recidivism rate for all persons released between 1960 and 1978 was between 27.5 and 37.8 when determined on the basis of a "three years at risk" study. The overall rate for the years 1960 through 1976 revealed an average recidivism rate of 36.2 after five years.

Non statistical evaluations are legion and easily discovered. All one need do is ask any sheriff or prosecuting attorney, or pursue the standard texts in corrections.

While the prisons are not responsible for the crime rate, *Historical Statistics of the United States*, Volume I and II, published by the U.S. Department of Commerce, reveals the following interesting statistics on the crime problem:

a)   Crime rates in the United States increased from 117/100,000 in 1957 to 459/100,000 in 1985.

b)   The nation's prison populations increased from 110/100,000 in 1950 to 201/100,000 in 1985.

c)   In Washington State, the end of the year population in prisons (all facilities) was approximately 3000 in 1950 and increased to 4382/ 100,000 in 1980.

142

(14)   More extensive study on the earlier prison experimentation with self government is to be found in Stastny and Tyrnauer: Who Rules the Joint? p.45-73, and Baker, J.E., The Right to Participate. p.25-80

(15)   In conversation on June 26, 1988, former superintendent Rhay confirmed that he sensed a lack of preparation for the RCG at the institution. He felt there had been insufficient time to get staff ready.

(16)   RCW 72.08.040 Duties of the Superintendent. The superintendent shall reside at the penitentiary, and it shall be his duty:

(1)   Under the order and direction of the department to prosecute all suits at law or in equity that may be necessary to protect the rights of the state in matters or property connected with the penitentiary and its management, such suits to be prosecuted by the attorney general, in the name of the department.

(2)   To supervise the government, discipline and police of the penitentiary, and to enforce all orders and regulations of the department in respect to the penitentiary. He shall keep a registry of the convicts, in which shall be entered the names of each convict, the crime for which he is convicted...

(3)   To perform other duties as may be prescribed by the department. 72.08.045 Temporary rules. When in his opinion an emergency exists, the superintendent may promulgate temporary rules for the governance of the penitentiary, which shall remain in effect until terminated by the director.

(17)   In a Special Edition of *Washington Public Employee*, under date of March 1970, the Washington Federation of State Employees revealed its pleasure at the accomplishments of the 41st Legislative Session. The publication's headline noted, "41st Legislature...It was Great!"

Editorializing on page 1, under the caption, "Responsible Unionism" the Federation noted:

"In many ways the 41st session of the Washington State Legislature was probably the most unusual in our state's history. One outstanding reason for this was the clear-cut demonstration of what responsible unionism can accomplish for state employees in the political arena."

The editorial noted that the favorable developments enjoyed by the union were the result of a carefully designed plan to find workable solutions to the problems of state government employment.

The Special Edition dealt extensively with the achievements to be enjoyed by the union under DSHS and quite accurately outlined the pertinent aspects of SB 52. These were referred to as the "one boss" responsible for hiring and firing, eliminating the appointing authorities existing throughout the departments. Also noted was the opportunity to request statewide bargaining units and the removal of the chief of personnel for the new department from the merit system. With this provision the union recognized its opportunity to hold the agency director fully responsible for the action of the agency director.

Also mentioned among the advantages to the union under SB 52 was the strength of the collective bargaining process.

(18)   The material quoted is from a Newsletter to the Presidents (of clubs and groups) which was prepared by the Resident Governmental Council and was forwarded to Mr. Smith by R.A. Freeman, Associate Superintendent at Walla Walla under date of September 9th, 1971. Additional negotiations were held on the day following Mr. Smith's surprise visit. At that meeting, G., of the Resident Governmental Council, suggested, (same Newsletter):

There is a need for Total Involvement, Staff and Inmates..... Sid Smith [then] asked, "To what degree are the Staff and Residents behind *self* government?"

..... Ed. By the way, replied that the residents were largely behind self government and should work with the staff but have not tried to do so hard enough....

Moses (Institution staff) tried to be slick, and asked "Does anyone know what the rules are?".... Bytheway replied, "The rules are Human rules, the rules of human decency....."

At this point, Sid Smith made the observation that none of us had put our whole heart in this thing, that we had all been shirking. He went on to say that if we wanted this thing to work, we had better "quit shirking and get on the ball"...

At this point, Sgt. Moses said he was going to tell his men, the ones who were lagging behind, the radicals, that they would either have to get on the ball or get off the hill. He made it plain that he was tired of their actions and was going to call them on the carpet.....

The RGC at this point stated that if Sgt. Moses would indeed go this far with the line officers, we would try to get our people to cooperate and make self government work....

At this point, Professor Lee Bowker, Citizens' Advisory Council said the RGC must take a harder line against the minority of rebels.....

Smith went on to say that if this works it will be great. It would be a giant step in penal history since, in his view, it was the only real prison reform instituted by and for the inmates....

(19)   In the June 26th meeting with Mr. Rhay, he commented that prior to DSHS, problems in the correctional institution were solved at the superintendent's level.

(20)   Roger Maxwell, former superintendent at Monroe, recalled that if one of the orders delivered by a deputy attorney general or a manager was not implemented promptly, there was an AG's opinion forthcoming in a day or so, ordering the action to be taken without further delay.

(21)   Stastny and Tyrnauer quote a Walla Walla resident:
"The administration just sort of divorced themselves from the whole situation because it was forced on them, so they indirectly uncooperated from the whole thing, if there's such a word, and they just sort of sat back and had a not-active resistance to it, you know. They doubted it would work...so, sure enough, it didn't work."

In our meeting on June 16, 1988, I discussed with former Superintendent Rhay the ill-disguised accusation that he had abdictated his responsibilities during this period of time and brought up the possibility that his veto power had not been used as extensively as it might have been. He did not agree that he had abdicated. Instead, he felt the veto power had been used extensively. He was, to be sure, much more impressed with his veto of union demands than of suggestions from the RGC. By way of example, he recalled that the union wanted to construct a chain link fence corridor from one guard station to the next "for protection" from the residents. Such construction would have been totally contrary to the basic hope of Reform calling for much closer communication with residents. The former Superintendent had "vetoed" the request; however, it was installed during the tenancy of a later superintendent.

Rhay indicated that he saw the union as always coming up with another absurd request. When their complaint related to their jobs being "unsafe," he invariably told them there were some risks inherent in employment in a prison system.

The former Superintendent was concerned about the allocation of his time as resistance to Reform got underway. He had many routine tasks to perform and new problems with which to deal. His position was complicated by the influx of individuals from Olympia who advised that they represented the office of the Secretary of DSHS and were there to tell him what to do. He found this very distressing since these individuals were laymen as regarded the corrections field, and their demands were often not compatible with good corrections programming.

Further demands were placed on the superintendent's time when due process was inserted into prison life. Attorneys were present in the institution on a full-time basis and paid from the institution's budget to defend the residents in the event disciplinary action was taken against them. Such actions became legal hearings.

That term, "legal hearing," also was applied to meetings between the prison administration and the union leadership in which the union was represented by its own lawyers and the administration was represented by an often young and inexperienced lawyer on the AG's staff.

Mr. Rhay's point was made quite clear: he had many responsibilities imposed on him which, unfortunately, had nothing to do with residents and the Reform Movement.

Rhay made mention of still another difficulty as he compared life under DSHS with the days under the Department of Institutions. In developing the guidelines for furloughs, the superintendents had submitted the product of their team effort. Their recommendations had called for the eligibility for furloughs to be dependent on a period of extended good behavior of the resident-applicant. But, these guidelines were rewritten by the assistant attorney general representing DSHS who left out that requirement. Later, an individual whose inappropriate behavior was predictable, killed a highway patrolman while on authorized leave from the institution. Experiences such as this left the superintendents feeling desperately alone, and unprotected without professional representation in the central office. When a convict escaped while on an outing under the Take-A-Lifer-to-Dinner program, the residents quickly mobilized to defend their superintendent.

(22)   The Take-a-Lifer-to-Dinner program was a local project at the Walla Walla institution. It called for an excursion into the community of a resident under life sentence to attend a dinner. The resident was accompanied by an institution staff person. Sometimes the trips away covered a considerable distance from the institution.

The project was not a part of the Reform Movement, nor was it a Departmental policy. Its legal status was extremely doubtful. I was not aware of the program until well after it had been established.

146

APPENDIX

I t is well known that the power struggle in the Washington correctional system eventually led to outbreaks of violence. The veto power, apparently not used for a time, was reasserted. Had it been employed earlier it might have been possible to create a more moderate rate of change in the transition from the old to a more expressive democratic society in the institution.

Since I was not an active participant in the reaction to the modern day reforms, I have chosen to complete this volume with some media comment about it, interspersed with other pertinent material of interest about the movement.

The following pages are devoted to various accounts of the Reform Movement and what happened later; in some instances much later. The comments are presented in a readable fashion and not necessarily in chronological order.

National support for the Reform Movement was clearly identified in a *Newsweek* article of November 1, 1971. The article paints a picture of what was happening in Reform and spells out the sense of hope that prevailed among the residents of the institutions.

PRISONS: Take a Giant Step

If the 1,154 inmates of Washington State Penitentiary are yardbirds of a very different plumage. Washington is not a typical maximum security prison. Last year, it granted its cons a measure of self-government unprecedented in American penology. Admirers hail the Washington experiment as the ounce of prevention for future Atticas; critics deride it as an invitation to anarchy. By any standard, Washington State Penitentiary, located in somnolent farm country on the outskirts of Walla Walla, is clearly the most innovative, liberal, maximum security prison anywhere in the U.S. It is a far cry from the days when unconscionable conditions earned it a reputation as the worst prison in the West and ignited two riots in 1955.

The turnabout at Washington results from pressure exerted by Dr. William Conte, a psychiatrist who had the chief responsibility for the state's prisons. Dissatisfied with prison reform, American-style, Conte sent the warden of the penitentiary, B.J. Rhay, on a scouting trip to Europe. Rhay was especially impressed with experiments in prison self-government by convicts in Denmark and Holland. Before the reforms, convicts could only complain bitterly over what they considered arbitrary and unduly severe punishment. Now, however, two council members are on hand at every disciplinary session, and while they are unable to vote, they can offer defense arguments — and ultimately protest the decisions directly to Superintendent Rhay...

The real concern, of course, is not simply returning prisoners to the streets but keeping them there. The recidivism rate in some U.S. prisons still runs as high as 70 percent. Historically, the nation's penitentiaries have functioned not as institutions of rehabilitation, but rather as what Ramsey Clark calls "factories of crime." It's far too soon to tell just what impact the reforms at Washington State Penitentiary will have, but many penal experts believe they are at the very least a giant step in the right direction...*Newsweek*, November 1, 1971

Upon my resignation from the Directorship of the Department of Institutions in July 1971, Governor Evans issued a press release expressing regret that I would be leaving. In addition, he listed accomplishments the Department had enjoyed during my tenure, referring to the state's favorable reputation in a number of areas, including a "national reputation for prison reforms, covering all aspects of corrections programming from architecture to attitude change."

The Seattle Times presented a series of articles published under the title, *"Does Nothing Work?,"* prepared by Ross Anderson. Excerpts from the *Times'* series follow with a few editorial and explanatory notes.

When under pressure to revert to the harsh and punitive days, Governor Evans asks, "How far back do we want to go?" (in an article in this series in late June 1975)

"If we're going back to a harsh-punishment concept, how far back do you want to go?" Gov. Dan Evans asks. "To the Salem-witchcraft days? Or to the Spanish Inquisition? Or maybe to the Moslem culture, where they cut off the thief's hand, or whatever part of the body (that) was at fault."

148

Like much of society, Evans has deep feelings about crime and criminals. But while others call for more punishment, the governor stands fast to his belief in "rehabilitation."

A new sense of futility — the "nothing works" syndrome — threatens to undermine what Evans considers to be vital reforms in the prison system and the entire justice system....

....The governor is aware that recent particularly sensational crimes have helped intensify public attitudes toward crime. He concedes that many blame the criminal-justice system for the problem...

Some of the frustrations of a cumbersome criminal-justice system have led people to the point where they want to say: "Nothing works, so let's just go back to harsh, corporal punishment.

"But in essence that's just a throwing up of the hands at a hard, social problem. And I can't bring myself to do that."

Evans became interested in prisons, he said, after he felt the state had made progress in updating mental health and other institutions.

"But we found corrections had been neglected because there is no natural constituency.

"I visited the various institutions, talking to the people. I realized this state was putting an awful lot of money into a correctional system which wasn't working very well." He said he decided it was not the concept of rehabilitation, but the outdated prison system which failed....Ross Anderson, *The Seattle Times*

In the "Does Nothing Work" series, an article entitled "Humanitarian or Permissive?" quoted this writer, the former Director of the Department of Institutions. The article is quoted extensively here because it presents the hope as well as the defense of the entire prison reform undertaking. This article appeared in *The Seattle Times* on June 25, 1975:

"Some call it the "Conte attitude." Some equate it with humanitarianism, others with permissiveness.

It is a set of high-sounding goals based on a view of human nature and set down in a tract-like pamphlet, *A Philosophy of Corrections*."

Dr. William R. Conte, then state director of institutions, outlined that philosophy here six years ago. Then he ordered an end to "strip cells" and mail censorship. He introduced telephones for convicts and partial self-government in the prisons.

With the staunch backing of a liberal Republican governor and an agreeable Legislature, he also established work release, training release and a broad furlough program.

The state was building the most liberal prison system in the nation.

Today, that system is in trouble. Prisons are more crowded and more violent. Drugs and weapons are more prevalent.

Some blame the permissiveness of the "Conte attitude" for the turn of events. The resident government at the state penitentiary at Walla Walla has been disbanded. Security has been tightened.

And Dr. Conte, who resigned four years ago, is a private psychiatrist in Tacoma.

"The most significant reform we attempted was a change in attitude", Conte said in a recent interview. "It was most important that we abandon the concept of prisoner and adopt the concept of resident."

Dr. Conte is a large man, with a broad-faced smile and bright, blue-gray eyes. He retains a strong pride in his corrections reforms and a silent sense of disappointment that some have been stalled.

"I sensed ill-feeling among residents of the institutions when I began," he recalled. "I perceived a certain danger if things were not changed. And it is quite evident today that we have not had an Attica because some of those residents recognized our attempts."

Dr. Conte left private practice in 1959 to join the late Dr. Garrett Heyns, then director of institutions. Dr. Conte succeeded him in 1966.

"We had our own philosophy in effect," he recalled. "The general guiding principle was that it had to be a humanitarian approach."

This broke down into several subpoints:

"First, we determined that to punish, to clobber a man has been proven ineffective in changing him, even if he was guilty of a horrible crime."

"Second, if we were to expect people to come out into society and improve their behavior, then we jolly well better set the stage in the institution.

"Third, we had a magnificent set of state statutes which speak consistently of rehabilitation, not punishment, and we interpreted that wording as the intent of the Legislature.

"And finally, we said that rehabilitation could only work by involving the offender in his own future."

Like most people, prison guards and other personnel did not welcome the prospect of change.

"We reached a point where we were discussing more than was reasonable with staff. We erred in trying to deal with too many negative feelings. In retrospect, it would have been better sometimes if we had said, 'This is the way it will be, boys!'"

His critics feel there were far deeper mistakes. Some of his ideas were naive, his reforms unworkable, they say. Others came too soon and too quickly before prison personnel were prepared to deal with them.

And some criticize Dr. Conte for his hasty resignation in 1971, shortly after his new policies had taken effect.

On January 3, 1975 the *Daily Olympian* carried an Associated Press article quoting extensively Superintendent Rhay:

State Pen Should Have Died With Dinosaurs

The state penitentiary here is "like a dinosaur and it should have gone out with them," says B.J. Rhay, the prison's warden.

"You don't manage it. If you asked me right now how the hell I manage it, I couldn't answer you. It somehow limps along.

I sure loved what I saw in Europe. Small prisons, some of them very secure and some of them much less secure.

"I saw a rapport between inmates and staff that anyone in America would love to see. I went to a staff college at The Hague where the state sent people to train them for their work in prisons.

"That's the direction we have to go."

A fear for the loss of reforms was expressed by two resident leaders at Walla Walla. One of the presidents of the Resident Governmental Council was quoted by Marjorie Jones, staff writer of *The Seattle Times* as stating:

> "These innovative and experimental programs, in spite of their
> high rate of success, (will disappear) one by one until they remain
> nothing but idealistic dreams of the advocates of penal reform."

This statement appeared in *The Seattle Times* in March 1979.

Still another president of the Resident Governmental Council called the Associated Press in late August 1979, a day or so after the 46-day lock down — the longest such event in the history of the Washington State penal system and said:

> Somebody, somewhere, has to do something about the union
> (the guards and employees). The union wants a crisis here so
> they can get rid of him (Prison Superintendent B.J. Rhay) and
> strengthen their hand.

A petition directed to a later governor of Washington, under date of April 12, 1977 and quoted here would never have been possible had it not been for Prison Reform. But a casual glance at the agenda items "respectfully submitted" for consideration suggests the document could have been created a century ago:

> Honorable Dixy Lee Ray, Governor
> State of Washington
> Office of the Governor
> Olympia, Washington
>
> Governor Ray:
>
> As you know, approximately 1400 inmates of the Washington State
> Penitentiary are presently deadlocked within the penitentiary of their
> own choice. This is the result of months of frustration with the
> administration and our attempts to negotiate conditions that exist.
>
> As President of the Resident Council, and working in conjunction
> with the club heads in the general population at the Washington State
> Penitentiary, we have submitted the enclosed requests to the administration here at the penitentiary....
>
> We are asking that you intercede in this matter in order to properly
> resolve those problem areas we have enumerated in the enclosed
> document...
>
> F. P., President
> Resident Council

The Petition

The Resident Council, as the elected representatives of the Washington State Penitentiary general population, in conjunction with representatives of the various clubs and organizations within the penitentiary, wish to present our grievances for the purpose of requesting an investigation of the problems encountered in the penitentiary, to an independent committee, appointed by Governor Ray, for this purpose...

...We feel a meeting such as is proposed is an appropriate step in our appeal for relief of our problems, which are alphabetically listed below....

1.   Classification

2.   Custody

3.   Jobs

4.   Medical Treatment

5.   Misuse of Funds

6.   Overcrowding

7.   Parole Board

8.   Racial Discrimination

9.   Resident Benefit Funds

10.   Segregation

11.   Time Structures

12.   Treatment Programs

13.   Visiting

14.   W.A.C. Violations

These areas will be presented in depth, with supportive
materials, at the time of the meeting with the committee.

F. P., President
W.S.P. Resident Council

In the fall of 1979, Christopher Bogan of *The Spokesman Review*, Spokane, Washington, produced a series of articles that ran during the month of November. These writings were the result of his tireless search for the facts about prison reform and its aftermath. He was objective and straightforward in his review and in his writing. Extensive excerpts from his writing are included here because they present another summary view of the Reform Movement.

On November 19, 1979, in the second of his articles, Mr. Bogan tells of an event that occurred on May 9, 1979 in which a number of residents of the Walla Walla institution took ten hostages. The "riot" was short-lived, but it did bring to the attention of the press a list of the residents' complaints. They were not unlike the complaints the central administration had heard when Garrett Heyns came to Washington in 1957, nor were they unlike those that had caused Governor Evans to endorse the efforts to improve conditions throughout the correctional institutions. These concerns are spelled out by Bogan as follows:

'...The primary demands included upgrading of the hospital and its staff, alleviation of overcrowding, especially in those areas where four men were living in two-man cells; separation of the mentally disturbed from the general prison population; transfer of prisoners under 21 to another prison; the halt of alleged beatings in the segregation unit; the upgrading of sanitary and other conditions in segregation; an investigation into the health standards of the prison kitchen; improvement of legal services and the prison law library; expansion and up-grading of rehabilitation programs; an increase in the prison's counseling staff and the institution of a program to screen applicants who apply to work as prison guards... — *Spokesman Review,* Nov. 19, 1979

The following Bogan excerpts were published on Nov. 21, 1979, under the title: "The Road to Reform Was Paved With Good Intentions, But it Led to a Crowded Hell"

The Washington State Penitentiary's recent history has often been written in blood. A Pandora's Box of violence opened during the seventies and still has not been closed. Prison officials claim one man ushered in this unprecedented age of violence. They blame Dr. William Conte, former director of Washington's Department of Institutions, for opening the door on the prison's current problems.

154

But Conte has a different view of the past. A social psychiatrist who now has left public office, he stands firmly by the changes he instituted 10 years ago at the prison.

The penitentiary's problems today cannot be understood without this chapter in the prison's history and Conte plays the leading role. Some will proclaim him a villain, and others a hero...

Consider the facts. Between 1960 and 1969, four homicides occurred inside the walls, and all were classified as "justifiable."

In the following 10 years, the prison took on the look of a morgue. From 1970 to 1979, there have been 23 murders and two other so-called "justifiable" homicides.

The lid on a Pandora's Box of violence was swung open at the Washington State Penitentiary in the 1970s and a tide of deaths, unprecedented in the prison's history, swept over the institution.

Why should one brief era in the penitentiary's 93-year history harbor such uncontrolled death and violence?

Many point their fingers accusingly at one man, Dr. William Conte. They blame him for being the one who lifted the lid on the prison's current problems.

It is naive to think one man can be made to bear the blame for the dark decade that has descended on the Washington State Penitentiary, but Dr. William Conte does present a key to understanding the prison and the monster that has grown in recent history within its walls.

Dr. Conte is the key not because he is a legitimate scapegoat but because he marks a crucial moment in the prison's history. To understand the present one must first unlock the past. Who then is William Conte and what is his place in the history of the Washington State Penitentiary?

A free-thinking, liberal social psychiatrist, Conte became director of Washington's Department of Institutions in 1966. Prior to this appointment, he served as supervisor of the Division of Mental Health.

Although he was a successful psychiatrist and had accomplished many things in the field of mental health, Conte's critics claim he knew nothing about administering the state's prison system and they passionately denounce him.

What did Conte do that has provoked such strong criticism from both present and former administrators at the state penitentiary?

In November 1970, he appeared before the media and state corrections officers to announce four changes in Washington's prison system. These changes, he said, were being made in an effort to humanize the state's prisons.

In retrospect, the changes seem rather unimportant, but former penitentiary superintendents, guards and administrators insist these changes were the first step in surrendering the prison to inmates and creating an environment that spawned death and violence.

"Here's a guy who came in through mental health and didn't know a damn about corrections," states B.J. "Robert" Rhay, the penitentiary's superintendent from 1957 until 1977. "And he made wide sweeping changes in corrections. He created the chaos we're suffering today."

Rhay is not alone in his opinion that Conte bears the blame. Robert Freeman, a 27-year veteran of the penitentiary and associate superintendent when he retired in 1976, stands right beside Rhay in this view.

"To me, Conte is the bad guy," Freeman says... "From then on (the initiation of his changes in 1970), it was just mass confusion and I don't think it has settled down yet. It's still confusion."

Yet Conte, who returned to private practice in Tacoma in 1971, is unimpressed and unsullied by these criticisms.

"I am not bothered by (these charges)," he fires back, "because if there were flaws in the programs that we envisioned, there has been plenty of time for some leadership to change them. When I hear that someone blames me 10 years later for the problems at Walla Walla today, I am reminded that some would blame Adam and Eve for all the sins of the world, and I can't be too much impressed by that."

Ten years later, here is what Conte did:

First, he abolished the use of "strip cells" inside the penitentiary. A holdover from the days when prisons were meant to be small Siberias, a strip cell is a dark room with a hole in the floor for a toilet and no other conveniences. Prisoners were incarcerated without clothes and served their time in an austere darkness.

"We abolished the strip cell and what this meant was that the man who was being punished for an infraction of the rules had to be treated like a human being," Conte states today.

"He could not be deprived of his clothes and isolated in a dark room with nothing but a hole in the floor through which human excrement was theoretically disposed of.

"I don't think you can rehabilitate a man if you reduce him to nothingness in the process of so-called rehabilitation. If one is angry with a man, you can destroy him and in my judgment strip cells destroyed the humanness of the individual who was subjected to the strip cells."

Conte's second reform was to install telephones inside the prison so that residents could make collect calls to their families. He stands by this reform, too.

"This," Conte notes, "meant that a man who was in prison, who had in fact misbehaved to the extent he was incarcerated and whose family had been deprived of his company, had the opportunity to call his wife collect and at least have some input and some support for her, while she was at home, often on public assistance, taking care of one or more children and doing so completely alone...For the man in prison to have that opportunity to have that input to his family was a very vital step forward."

Next, Conte abolished prison censorship of ingoing and outgoing mail. This reform particularly panicked the penitentiary staff, which worried that inmates would be able to smuggle weapons and contraband into the prison. But in Conte's view, he was restoring a basic constitutional right to the inmates.

The fourth reform, which was the most specific and the most sweeping, authorized the creation of a resident governmental council inside the prison. Prisoners were to be given a hand in shaping their own destiny inside the walls.

"It concerned me deeply," Conte recalls, "to think that a man, who was already troubled and in trouble, was in no way being included in the plans for his own future. It concerned me even more deeply that a man who came to the correctional facility with the idea that he was to learn how to behave and to associate with others and how to respect the person and property of others was being abused and being made to feel more bitter."

"The purpose of the council," Conte recalls, "was to give the man in prison an opportunity to learn something of the process of representative government because, after all, we were preparing him to return home.

"Many people who are in prison have lived at the periphery of the law all their lives. They have come from a walk of life which hasn't cared very much about what the law says and when they went to prison, everything was decided for them.

"By establishing the resident governmental council, the men in prison had representation. Their ambitions and their complaints could be presented through formal channels in the same way Mr. and Mrs. Average Citizen bring their needs and wants to the attention of the city council, or the county commission, or the state legislature."

Looking back, Conte says he believes our prisons were returning men to society with more anger and hatred inside them than when they entered prison.

"I felt that the taxpayers were being gypped," he says. "Ultimately, they paid the price of the man's trial and the price of the rehabilitation of the individual, and what they were getting back at the end of the incarceration was an angry man who was more dangerous to society than when he went in..."

Prison officials were stunned when Conte mandated his reforms. In retrospect, most admit the changes were not that dramatic, but they did mark a crucial shift in attitude.

Suddenly, the prisoners had rights and were not subject to the indiscriminate orders and power that formerly existed. The liberalism of the sixties had finally made its way into the penitentiary.

There was little prison administrators and staff could do if they didn't like the reforms. The orders came from the top. They could quit or swallow hard.

Most swallowed hard and instituted the reforms at the penitentiary; yet the spirit with which they did this was lackluster. It was almost as if the prison staff had said, "We'll do as we're told and let Conte hang himself."

This attitude became most apparent in the handling of the resident councils. The prisoners were allowed to form clubs and organize their governmental councils, but they had little help or knowledge of just what to do.

"The convicts tried to form clubs and find direction," one inmate recalls, "but they didn't have anyone to give them direction. I believe we had too much freedom, because we didn't do nothing. You wouldn't work your way towards nothing."

What happened then was that over time the clubs evolved into prison gangs. Reflecting on the past, Associate Superintendent James Cummings says one of the biggest mistakes the administration made was allowing each group to have a club area. Suddenly the groups had "turf" or "territory," which strengthened their sense of power and autonomy.

Each club area became a small kingdom and inmates learned quickly not to trespass over certain grounds. It reached the point, guards say, where individual officers would not go into places like the bikers' shop without the support of several other guards...

In truth, there are no smoking guns in this chapter of the prison's history. There are victims and many of them, but the victims are dead and gone.

What remains are the problems of an institution that lost direction and control. The problems are here and now.

— *Spokesman-Review*, November 22, 1979

In truth, prison clubs were never a part of the Reform Movement.

Another Bogan article in the same series was entitled: "Society's Executioner: Forces Of History Which Led to Crime"

...Prisons do not exist apart from the society which builds them. They reflect the society, just as the society is history's mirror. The problems of the Washington State Penitentiary are the legacy of the past as surely as they will become the foundation ground of the future....

With World War II and the Korean War lying in the country's past, Americans looked into the 1950s as a new era of normalcy and prosperity. The men had left the battlefields to return home to make and raise families. Thus, the 1950s marked the largest surge in population in the country's history.

While the sixties were marked by a cultural revolution and the seventies have been dubbed the "Me Decade," the fifties were years of procreation, the decade of the "baby boom"...

This baby boom in the 1950s spawned a generation, criminologists say, that would come of age in the 1970s. These children of the fifties would be between 17 and 25 years old in the seventies and crime experts say this is the age when people are most likely to get into trouble with the law. They call it the "at-risk population," and FBI records show that in 1977, 73 percent of the people arrested throughout the country were under 25 years old. Indeed, 59 percent of this criminal pool was under the age of 21.

When the seventies arrived, this at-risk population swelled to numbers greater than ever before...

Labor analysts in Olympia report that the state's unemployment rate soared upwards in the seventies, just as it did throughout the country.

In 1968...only 4.9 percent of the state's total labor force were out of work, but only three years later 10.1 percent of the state's workers had joined the rolls of the unemployed. A total of 142,000 people had no jobs in 1971.

With the state's population steadily rising, the labor force expanded too. This meant that a continued, even if steady, unemployment trend would turn more people out of work.

In 1975...the unemployment rate was 9.6 percent, .3 percentage points lower than in 1971, but because the labor force was so much greater, more people were actually unemployed than in 1971. A total of 147,000 people swelled the unemployment rolls in 1975....

In the years reaching from 1968 to 1977, Dave Cassens, FBI spokesman, notes the national crime rate increased by an incredible 63 percent. Violent crimes throughout the country sky-rocketed up almost 70 percent and property crimes jumped 62 percent.

In Washington state, FBI statistics tell the same crime story. In 1968, Cassens points out, Washington residents were the victims of 77,700 crimes. A total of 91 percent, or 71,000, were property crimes and nine percent, or 7,000, were violent personal crimes.

By 1978, however, Washington residents were victimized 210,000 times — a staggering 270 percent increase in crime over the course of the decade. Property crimes had risen to 195,800, or 93 percent, of all incidents and violent crimes jumped up to 14,700 incidents, or seven percent, of all state crime.

Against this backdrop of rising crime rates, local police departments have been pushed to the wall by public outrage. As a result, the number of arrests and convictions for crime have risen significantly.

Overcrowding is certainly one of the most urgent problems at the state penitentiary.

When American Correctional Association officers toured the state penitentiary this summer, they found the conditions inside the walls were "intolerable"...

Between 400 and 500 inmates should be removed from Washington State Penitentiary within the immediate future, the ACA experts stated bluntly....

With the majority of inmates living in four-man cells that are about 9-1/2 feet by 12-1/2 feet, it is no wonder fights have broken out...

The crowded environment at the Washington State Penitentiary, created by a host of social factors, has become an executioner in its own right. The 23 murders of the 1970s bear witness to this fact.

— *Spokesman-Review*, November 22, 1979

In *The Spokesman-Review* on November 24, 1979, under the headline, "Fury in the Soul: Night of Terror", Mr. Bogan continued his series on Walla Walla and the prison riot which erupted on July 7, 1979. He refers to inmates who:

...rioted and wantonly destroyed their prison cells. In response to this senseless violence, a prison tactical force, using riot sticks and brute force, herded the inmates from their cells into a walled yard, where the men remained for the next 44 days. It was a night of terror for nearly all involved, a night which will be remembered as a savage spectacle of violence and inhumanity.

He notes that the riot beginning on July 7 is a moment in prison history which will long be remembered, but "the preceding days are what should first be recalled." Then, his article continues:

After three weeks on lockdown, prison Superintendent James Spalding ordered a prison-wide shake-down to seize all contraband. Every cell in the penitentiary was to be searched.

A shakedown squad entered Eight Wing on Thursday, July 5. It was the last cell block to be searched. The searches took all afternoon and then continued through Friday, July 6. Here is where the natural tension was suddenly stretched to a breaking point.

An inmate calls his cell his "house" and decorates it to give an otherwise barren cage some character and warmth. Some men put up posters and family pictures, while others hung curtains around toilets and painted on the walls. Many of these decorative touches were against prison regulations but for a long time they had been overlooked by guards.

That time was over now.

Once before, in another shakedown of Eight Wing, guards had uncovered a zip gun, seven rounds of ammunition, a dozen knives, needles, dope and marijuana. No one knew what they'd find this time and the guards searched with vigilantes' zeal.

Bill Cross was the first guard in the prison's 93-year history ever to be murdered directly by inmates. His death enraged the guards. Several officers on shakedown duty began referring to themselves as the "Cross Revenge Squad."

The shakedown squad usually searched two cells at a time. They moved the residents — four to each cell — out of their houses and locked them in a storage closet. The summer heat was oppressive. Many inmates had stripped down to their underwear. In their underwear, then, they were led to the storage closet, where they remained for nearly an hour as guards searched their cells.

When finally they returned to their cells, they were horrified. Their clothing lay in a heap on the floor. Personal letters, legal documents, and family pictures were gone. Many televisions, radios, tape recorders and other personal items had been taken. In some cells, even mattresses had been removed. Only blankets lay atop the bunkbeds.

Some were stunned, some unbelieving, all were outraged. Guards inventoried most confiscated items and stowed them in boxes outside the cells. But many inmates looked onto the cell tier to see letters and pictures of loved ones ripped, torn and trampled on the floor.

"They took everything out and they expected you to be like you were before," remarked M., a former Eight Wing resident. "When people walked in, they got really pissed off. I had family pictures taken. I have a brother who is dead and I'm never going to get another picture of him. We had a picture drawn on the wall and they put an 'X' on it like Zorro. They were just being crazy...they were trying to take everybody's pride, that's what they were trying to do."

The handling of the shakedown caused more bitterness and hatred in the residents than the administration could ever have guessed.

"You've taken all this stuff away from them and therefore you've created a vacuum in which violence thrives," observed inmate M.F. "You've got nothing but bitterness in that place.

"Picture yourself in a cell for five years and your only contact is with your family through letters they have sent you. Then an officer comes into your house and tears up your pictures and throws your clothes over the (tier) side. That hurts, and it happens..."

Angry, bitter, stunned, confused, the men talked in their cells that night of the day's events and then they went to bed about midnight.

Like the bad taste in their mouths, the bitterness was still with them in the morning. They had been locked in their cells for three weeks. Many had gone 22 days without a shower. The July heat was blistering. They learned to wash like birds, splashing themselves with water from their cell sinks. And now, after the shakedown, many inmates were without toilet paper, soap or towels.

The combination of events was too much. It rubbed residents' nerves raw. Rational thought processes suddenly seemed to break down and infantile responses took their place.

— *Spokesman-Review*, November 24, 1979

And the riot ensued.

The actions of the "guards" reported here are incredible. These persons were the individuals who were to be the vanguards of the Reform Movement. They had been depended upon to understand, to be compassionate and to rehabilitate the offender.

Bogan's writings in the series continued under the title of "The Weapon of the Guards":

> Members of the Washington State Penitentiary's special tactical squad, usually known as the "Riot Team," carry riot sticks when on emergency duty. It was a riot stick like this one that inmate Carl Harp charges prison guards used to sodomize him.

> ...What happened in the segregation unit on July 7 (1979)?

> The incident began around noon, when lunch was not served to the segregation unit residents. About 1 p.m., inmate G. shouted from his cell to the shift sergeant, asking why they hadn't been fed.

> Sgt. Harold Lee informed G. no lunch was being served today because guards were trying to straighten out the mess in Eight Wing.

> G. either didn't hear this information or he misunderstood it, because state investigators found that he informed other residents they were being punished for the riot in Eight Wing and henceforth they would receive only two meals each day.

> This misinformation was never corrected by the officer on duty. Had it been, an incident might well have been avoided.

> Hungry and without the prospect of a meal, the inmates began banging on their cells and shouting. When they grew tired of this, G. shouted again to Sgt. Lee and threatened that if the residents didn't get fed they would tear up their cells.

> As H., a segregation resident, later put it: "We decided if we had to pay for what someone else had done, we might as well do the same thing."

> Sgt. Lee responded that he knew how the inmates felt but that tearing up their cells would do no good. G. reportedly passed this on as, "They say they don't care."

To protest, several inmates decided to tear up their cells after the evening meal. By breaking loose the cell's stool, an inmate could use it as a weapon to destroy the sink, toilet and cell bunk.

In cell B19, resident C. a big, tough man, had jumped the gun. After ripping loose the cell stool, C. knew he would be removed from his cell. He decided to destroy his cell before the others.

At 3:35 P.M., when six to eight officers arrived at C. cell to move him to another unit, they found C. with the stool in his hands and saying, "Come and get me, mother f———."

Officer Parley Edwards, then president of the guards' union, talked to C.and calmed him down. He was handcuffed and moved peacefully to the prison's mental health wing...

After dinner...an angry pounding began in the segregation unit. Inmates were tearing up their cells as they had planned.

...One by one, the inmates were restrained and handcuffed to their cell bars. Some force was used. It's hard to say how much. With four, five and six guards jamming into tiny one-man cells to overcome a single prisoner, with riot sticks, protective 'sapp' gloves, and mace hanging heavy in the air, people were inevitably knocked, shoved and rocked about in the sardine-like cells.

The four inmates were left handcuffed to their cell bars and then the riot team went to get C. He had broken out of his handcuffs and trashed another cell...

...C. was taken to the head of segregation's A tier and bound with two sets of handcuffs in a spread-eagle position with his back to the bars.

Then, C.claims, two officers spread his legs apart and kicked him in the testicles and hit him with a riot stick.

"I heard another guard say, 'Well, when we get done tonight, we'll be able to have real good sex with the old lady,' C. states bitterly. "That's a quote, word for word, what this punk said."

At this point, early in the evening, the prison administration was for the first time notified of the trouble in segregation.

"In light of the destruction of Eight Wing on the previous night," state officials later remarked in their special report, "the investigative team found this unbelievable and one of the many examples of inadequate and inaccurate communication between the administration and the staff and vice versa."

The five inmates would be moved from segregation to strip cells in another part of the building. But in the process, state investigators found, they were beaten with batons, punched, kicked, maced and generally roughed up...

With the start of this rough treatment, Carl Harp began shouting at the riot squad members. He protested in sharp abusive terms the brutal treatment of the other inmates.

Guards told Harp to shut up, but he did not. Then, Harp claims, officer Patrick Nugent tried to poke him with a nightstick through the cell bars. Nugent, on the other hand, claims Harp tried to hit him and he parried with his baton.

In either event, Harp grabbed the riot stick thrust at him and a pulling match ensued. Harp was doomed to be the loser whoever won this tug of war. He was ordered to join the others being moved...

Harp had a reputation for being accomplished in the martial arts and he was seen to be a troublemaker because he was extremely vocal in his political views damning prisons...

According to Harp, here is what happened: "They were on me immediately with sticks and fists, calling me a political prisoner, a jailhouse lawyer, a punk, a hostage taker and a sniper. The lieutenant in charge maced me and encouraged the beating with the majority of these remarks and by saying, 'Want to file a lawsuit?'

"They beat and dragged me to the floor and put me face down and then beat and kicked me while they handcuffed me violently behind the back. They stomped on my whole exposed body from the head down.

"Once on the floor they started talking about me being involved in an organization known as 'Men Against Sexism,' a gay and anti-sexist organization at Walla Walla, and calling me a punk and one of them wanted to f——— me to see what it was like. Suddenly my pants were yanked down to my knees and the guard who wanted to f——— me rammed his riot stick between my legs and up into my rectum and then played gear shift with the stick in me. I screamed when it entered me. The pain was gross."

Harp later would take a polygraph test to verify his claim that he'd been raped. He was asked the question, "Did you lie when you said a guard shoved a night stick up your rectum?" To this question, Harp answered, "No," and the polygraph test indicated this was a truthful statement...

The Spokesman-Review's investigation has raised some doubt with the state's conclusion that the medical examination convincingly proved Harp was not raped.

Dr. Saw's medical report states a "rectal exam showed a 2-1/2 cm. laceration of the anus at the left anterior quadrant extending to the submucosa with minimal bleeding."...

... the rape charge drew quick response. Spalding immediately suspended with pay 12 guards involved in the segregation incident. The rape charge and reports of prison mistreatment drew a shocked response from many citizens and administrators in state government. A state ordered investigation, led by Brooks Russell from the Attorney General's Office and James Jackson from the Department of Licensing, with the help of the Walla Walla City Police, was quickly launched...

When Jackson and Russell completed their investigation into the matter three weeks later, they concluded the incident occurred because of four primary factors:

- Inadequate or non-existent psychological screening of correctional officers when hired.

- Inadequate basic training for guards and almost non-existent in-service training.

- A total lack of screening of special assignment personnel, particularly the riot team.

- The decision to call in the riot squad was made upon fragmented and inaccurate information.

"There seems to be an attitude along the line of 'We' and 'Them,' and an opportunity for the Wes to prevail over the Thems seemed to be something desirable,'" Jackson and Russell observed.

In summary, the two state investigators concluded correctional officers were overworked and poorly trained. A continual failure of communication greased the skids for an incident that might otherwise have been avoided. Poor leadership among correctional officers also contributed to the staff's failure to respond professionally when a tense situation arose.

> The events in the segregation unit might have been avoided. Instead, they became a nightmare and headache for the prison and its staff..."

— *Spokesman-Review*, November 25, 1979

Indeed: "we" and "them." Obviously, not an environment in which rehabilitation could take place.

(The guards involved in the July 1979 abuses were suspended and several were later dismissed.)

In May, 1980, a suit brought by the residents of the Walla Walla institution came before the Federal Court, Judge Jack Tanner presiding. Stastny and Tyrnauer report the outcome of those proceedings in *Who Rules The Joint?*, p.112:

> In closing arguments for the inmates' side, Attorney Steve Scott expressed the heart of the plaintiff's case: "The prisoners of the penitentiary at Walla Walla came to this court to show that the defendants (the state officials) have subjected the prisoners to even below the basic minimum of human decency."

After the trial concluded, state officials quite openly expected the worst...On May 24, Tanner announced his decision orally: "The totality of conditions at Walla Walla is cruel and unusual punishment beyond any reasonable doubt."

William R. Conte (May 26, 1921 —)

William R. Conte was born on May 26, 1921, in Grand Forks, North Dakota. His father was an accomplished musician of Italian heritage.

His mother, a concert pianist, was from Appleton, Minnesota. His parents were deeply involved in teaching and they regularly performed in concerts, both individually and together.

Dr. Conte was raised in an academic setting. Throughout his childhood, his father held teaching positions in music at Wesley College, University of North Dakota; Oklahoma Baptist University, first as faculty member and then as Dean of Fine Arts; and finally, as a member of the faculty at the University of Wichita, Wichita, Kansas.

Dr. Conte received his B.A. degree from the University of Wichita in 1942 and his M.D. degree from the Vanderbilt University School of Medicine in 1945. Upon completing medical school he served a one-year internship in medicine and surgery at the Pennsylvania Hospital in Philadelphia, Pennsylvania, during which time he met and married Suzanne Keay, a registered nurse. He served his military duty as a naval medical officer stationed at the Veteran's Administration Hospital in Wichita, Kansas, from 1946 to 1948.

While serving at the Veterans Hospital, Dr. Conte was the Associate Chief for Psychiatric Services. His talent for treating psychiatric patients and his satisfaction in working with them there sparked a life-long interest in and dedication to the field of psychiatry.

He pursued his dedication first as a trainee and then as a member of the faculty of the Department of Psychiatry, University of Colorado, School of Medicine. In 1951 he became the Assistant Administrator of the Colorado Psychopathic Hospital. He was certified by the American Board of Psychiatry and Neurology in 1952.

Between 1952 and 1957, Dr. Conte was in the private practice of Psychiatry in Greeley, Colorado. During this period he became

169

increasingly concerned over the inaccessibility of psychiatric treatment to those who were less than affluent. This led to an interest in the then new concept of community psychiatric services. As a result, he accepted a position as the Director of the Mental Health Clinic of Greeley's Weld County Health Department where he became a pioneer in the field of community services. His belief in and hope for community services led him to found and serve as the Director of the Larimer County Mental Health Facility at Fort Collins, Colorado and, perhaps more importantly, it brought him in contact with the Menninger Foundation and Drs. Karl and Will Menninger.

The Menningers were pioneers in the field of mental health and shared Dr. Conte's desire to make psychiatric services available to the less fortunate. Conte developed a particularly close friendship with Dr. Will Menninger finding in him, at once, a "kindred spirit" and a mentor. Will Menninger instilled in the younger physician a very liberal and democratic approach to treatment, a firm belief in staff training and teaching, and a belief that there is no problem that cannot be solved.

That same desire to reach more people in need of psychiatric treatment resulted in an interest in the state's role in providing a variety of social services and, more specifically, state mental hospital services. He left his private practice in 1957 and began searching for opportunities to participate in state mental health programs. During this period, he accepted a position as Associate Professor of Psychiatry at the University of Texas' Southwestern Medical School in Dallas. Then, in 1959, the opportunity he had been waiting for came when he was offered and accepted a position as the first Supervisor of the Division of Mental Health for the Washington State Department of Institutions.

Conte was brought to Washington State by Dr. Garrett Heyns, then Director of the Department of Institutions. Dr. Heyns had a long and distinguished career in teaching and in the field of corrections. Heyns and Conte had independently concluded that Washington State, with its progressive Governor and Legislature, provided a unique opportunity for the advancement of state-provided social services. In particular, Washington State had demonstrated an interest in improving the care and treatment of those in state mental institutions as well as an interest in the rehabilitation of those in state correctional facilities. In Dr. Heyns, Conte found, again, both a "kindred spirit" and a mentor.

Dr. Heyns was a man of vast experience, both in and out of public service, and an individual with tremendous administrative ability. The two men shared a strong commitment to providing care for those who were less fortunate and to improving the quality of the service and treatment provided to those who were in the care of the

170

state. They also shared an academic, liberal, and democratic approach towards their endeavors. They worked together as a team from 1959 until 1966, with Conte concentrating on the state's mental health programs and Heyns concentrating on the state's correctional system.

During Dr. Conte's tenure as Supervisor of the Department's Division of Mental Health, all three state mental hospitals received accreditation by the Joint Commission on Hospital Accreditation, the first time in state history all three state hospitals were accredited at the same time. The hospital programs established by Conte had a strong academic and research orientation and soon they became training centers for students in medicine, psychiatry, nursing, social work, occupational therapy, and public administration. The success of these treatment programs is most clearly measured by the markedly shortened hospital stay for patients and the dramatic reduction in population which the state psychiatric hospitals experienced.

In 1966, at the age of 75, Dr. Heyns retired from state service and Governor Daniel J. Evans appointed Dr. Conte to succeed Heyns as the Director of Institutions. At that time, the Director was responsible for the supervision, administration, treatment, training, and research relating to thirty-two state institutions including: adult and juvenile correctional institutions, mental hospitals, schools for the retarded, schools for the blind and deaf, veteran's homes, and a variety of community programs.

Justice James Dolliver of the Washington State Supreme Court served as Chief of Staff for Governor Evans. He recalls that Conte was an outstanding administrator who, through his strong professional abilities, earned the loyalty of his staff and the respect of his colleagues.

As Director of the Department of Institutions and with the firm support of Governor Evans, Conte took up where Heyns left off and began to implement programs which were, nationally, at the cutting edge of reform regarding the care, treatment, and rehabilitation of residents of state correctional programs.

The professional and treatment orientation of Conte's approach to corrections is perhaps most clearly reflected in his Philosophy of Corrections discussed in this volume. It is, no doubt, his greatest contribution to the field.

Justice Dolliver describes Conte's philosophy as a realization that correctional systems must strive to rehabilitate residents and prepare them for their inevitable return to society. Dolliver points out that Conte's efforts relating to resident participation marked, in the State of Washington, the culmination of a national reform movement in the field of corrections that actually began in the early twentieth century.

As a testimony to the work of both Conte and Heyns, Dr. Karl Menninger, in an address to the Washington State Legislature on February 6, 1970, stated: "To the scenic beauties of Washington must now be added the beauty of the best correctional program in the United States." In 1971, the Washington State Legislature created the Department of Social and Health Services, an umbrella agency, under which were placed a number of existing agencies, including the Department of Institutions. Dr. Conte served as Deputy Secretary of the new Department of Social and Health Services from January until July of 1971 at which time he retired from state service and established a private practice in Tacoma, Washington.

In addition to the teaching positions noted, Conte has taught at the School of Occupational Therapy, Colorado A & M College in Fort Collins, Colorado (1952-59), the Denver University School of Social Work (1951-52), and the University of Washington, Department of Psychiatry, 1960-69. He has held numerous lecturer, consultant, and advisory positions in various schools of psychiatry, psychology and counseling, and occupational therapy.

Dr. Conte has served on a number of committees including the Committee on Therapy of the American Psychiatric Association and the Advisory Committee to the National Occupational Therapy Association. He has also served as a Member of the Board of the American Corrections Association. He is a life fellow of The American Psychiatric Association, a member of The Washington State Mental Health Association, The Group for the Advancement of Psychotherapy, and The Washington Corrections Association. He is a past member of the American Geriatrics Association, The American Academy of Religion and Psychiatry, The American Medical Association, and The National Correctional Administrators Association.

Dr. Conte has over fifty publications to his credit covering such areas as: psychiatric diagnosis and treatment, occupational therapy, state mental health and correctional programs, community services programs, social psychiatry, and administration.

Both Dr. Conte and Dr. Heyns felt strongly the importance of recording program developments. As a result, a comprehensive, if not voluminous record of their work now resides in the Washington Room of the Washington State Library, to which will now be added a copy of this volume.

The Contes have four children and live in Olympia, Washington.

Kenan R. Conte.

172

Garrett Heyns (Sept. 21, 1891 — Nov. 3, 1969)

Garrett Heyns was born in a rural village outside Grand Rapids, Michigan on September 21, 1891. He was the third in a family of nine children. His father was, at the time of his birth, a minister in the Christian Reformed Church, and Garrett's schooling reflected the many moves his father made from one parish to another in South Dakota, Minnesota, Illinois, and Michigan. After his father became a professor in 1901 at the Calvin College and Seminary in Grand Rapids, Michigan, the family settled down for good.

These early days played an important role in our father's life. It was the period of the Cleveland depression. There was little market for farm products. Long periods of drought added to the poverty of the parishioners, among whom the family lived. Much of his lifelong sympathy for the poor and the neglected had its origin in these experiences.

Garrett Heyns completed his secondary education in Grand Rapids, Michigan at the preparatory school conducted by Calvin College. After two years of work at Calvin College, he taught elementary school to earn enough money to go to the University of Michigan. He received his AB from that institution in 1915, his MA in 1916.

After receiving his Master's degree, he taught in high schools in Royal Oak, Michigan, Blandinsville, Illinois, and Hull, Iowa. During the summers he pursued his doctoral work. His thesis was a study of the origins of democratic institutions in France and dealt specifically with the Estates General of 1484. He was awarded the Ph.D degree in medieval history from the University of Michigan in 1927. Our father never lost his enthusiasm for history, for libraries, and for scholarship. We remember fondly being told stories of British kings and queens; we learned about fairy tales much later, and not from him.

173

Another significant experience overlapped with this period of post graduate training under strenuous conditions. Undoubtedly he aspired to teach history at a college or university after completing his Ph.D. Jobs of this sort, however, were rare in the late 20s and early 30s, and Garrett devoted himself to administrative posts in elementary and secondary schools. He founded and served as principal of a private high school, the Western Academy, in Hull, Iowa.

He also served as superintendent of schools in Holland, Michigan. These schools were private in the sense that they were maintained and supported by the parents of the children, most of whom were members of the Christian Reformed Church. Only much later, in the 1950s, did he teach at the university level; for several years he taught a seminar in criminology at the University of Michigan.

The period of administrative work in elementary and secondary education extended from the early 1920s until 1937. It was, like his early childhood, a time of hardship. The Great Depression came to the farms of the Midwest in the 20s and to the industrial Midwest in the 30s — almost exactly accompanying Garrett's move from Iowa to Michigan. The schools with which he worked suffered the hardships of the parents who formed the societies that governed the schools. Unemployment was common; teacher salaries were low and the society frequently was unable to meet the payroll.

This period, too, it seems to us, was particularly significant in developing the characteristics we recognized and appreciated in him. He was a frugal man and learned to get along with improvisations. He learned that large accomplishments call for dedicated and highly motivated people. His sensitivity to the need for mutual respect among the members of organizations had its origins in those experiences with organizations under stress. Those days also stamped him forever as an educator — committed to the belief that education was important for self improvement and for the health of the society. It made him think first of education as a means to deal with society's problems.

During this period, Garrett Heyns was an active member of a group of Christian educators whose central purpose it was to search out the implications of a Christian commitment for one's professional life. He and his colleagues, fellow graduates of Calvin College, came from a variety of occupations, conducted seminars, wrote papers, and gave speeches on this subject. They believed that a religious commitment involved more than church attendance and other rituals of religious life; Christianity, for them, required a deep concern with the problems of society and the well being of its members. This interest, strengthened and sharpened during his thirties and early forties through his work with children and with struggling institutions, characterized his life and remained one of his major motivations.

The year 1937 began the next major phase in his life, a period of twenty years in corrections in the State of Michigan. Frank Murphy, at that time Michigan's Governor, and later U.S. Attorney General, and later still, Justice on the U.S. Supreme Court, decided to reorganize the prison system. What formerly had been a major part of the "spoils system" was to be put under the civil service; former law enforcement personnel were to be replaced by educators, and the philosophical emphasis was to move from punishment and segregation to reeducation and rehabilitation. Garrett Heyns was one of the first educators to be chosen; he was appointed Warden of the Ionia Reformatory, an institution for young, male first-offenders.

There was a great deal of ferment in the fields of prison, probation and parole. Indeterminate sentences became more frequent and as a consequence, a professional parole system had to be developed, including parole boards and parole supervisors. Prisons became differentiated with respect to the inmates housed. Young first offenders were housed together, under appropriate conditions of security. Classification boards, consisting of academic and vocational educators, psychologists, and psychiatrists, assigned inmates to schools or jobs deemed to be appropriate and therapeutic. Progress was monitored by these boards regularly and ultimately parole hearings were recommended. Academic and vocational schools were established and work assignments in the various shops were made into apprenticeship training whenever possible. We remember our father returning from trips to Detroit with machine tools for the vocational school that he had scrounged from companies in the area.

Inmates who had received paroles were not allowed to leave the institutions until they had jobs. Often prison employees and parole officers helped to locate these positions.

We are not suggesting that none of these practices existed before this time, nor that they became universal soon after. Indeed, many of these practices were and remain controversial. But they were the ideas that dominated our father's life and implementing them intelligently was his absorbing preoccupation.

After two years as Warden, the wardenships were removed from the protection of Civil Service, and he was replaced by a political appointment. A year later, he was made the state's Director of Corrections. After eight years he served as Chairman of the Parole Board (when the directorship was again eliminated as a Civil Service position). Some time later, he returned to the Ionia Reformatory as

Warden. This job gave him direct contact with the process of rehabilitation and was clearly the job he enjoyed most.

During the Michigan period, Garrett Heyns was active on the national corrections scene. He served as President of the American Prison Association, of the American Correctional Association, and of the American Parole Association. He wrote articles for professional journals and spoke at regional, national and international meetings on corrections subjects. His records show more than fifty such publications and speeches from 1942 to 1968. During World War II, he served on the corrections task force of the President's Commission on Law Enforcement and Administration of Justice.

Garrett Heyns' final career change resulted from the invitation extended to him by Governor Albert D. Rosellini to come to the State of Washington to be the Director of the Department of Institutions. He was 66 at the time, and was to spend the next nine years in that position. He resigned one week short of his 75th birthday.

There is no need for us to discuss this period in his life; indeed, this book, written by his friend and esteemed colleague, William R. Conte, deals expertly with the visions, the problems, and achievements of that chapter.

For us, as is the case with all fortunate children, our father's life adds up to more than chronology. We were a close family and, for much of our lives, he and his work were the focus of our attention. From this intimate knowledge and frequent contact, we became deeply conscious of certain characteristics that we came to revere and which people, like us, close to him came to expect, admire, and emulate. We think of four in particular. The first is his enormous integrity.

He was not manipulative; he respected others, listened to them; his word was credible and his behavior was predictable. Friends and foes alike had no reason to doubt his intentions or question his conduct. The second — his sense of fairness, his understanding of the desire of everyone to be treated fairly. He was concerned with the inequities of our society, but he was also deeply sensitive to the importance of fairness in our interpersonal relations. We were also aware of the third trait — his determination. He started school in Iowa; he got his Ph.D under trying circumstances, he tackled the problems in the field of corrections. These are but a few of the examples of the depth of his motivation and his willingness to persist toward worthy goals. And finally, closely related to this unwillingness to be daunted, was his willingness to take risks. We can remember that almost every one of the career changes we have mentioned involved uncertainties, risks of considerable magnitude. They meant leaving secure and predictable situations for the unknown and the unpredictable. And, in each of these jobs there were choices to be made that required new and untried solutions to tough problems, often exposing the institutions and the causes to severe public criticism. These decisions he made thoughtfully, prayerfully, and then his energies were directed toward implementing them intelligently. There was no time wasted in aimless reconsideration.

Life with our father was a great privilege. He was a good parent, loving and interested in us. He was a fine husband. He had an intelligent and supportive partner in Rosa, our mother and his wife, and he appreciated the role she played in his life. They had a long and successful marriage. He was a man of honor, wisdom, determination and courage, devoted to the service of mankind. That is the way he seemed to us and that, we believe, is the way he looked to those outside the family who worked and played with him.

Finally, we both want to thank Dr. Conte for this book. It covers a crucial time in the history of the State of Washington and makes an important contribution to public understanding. The book is also a labor of love on Dr. Conte's part and we are grateful to him for his generous descriptions of the role of Garrett Heyns. Their partnership was a fruitful and happy one and, we venture to say, the State of Washington has been the principal beneficiary of their efforts.

Roger W. Heyns
Jacqueline Heyns Rudeen
January, 1989

EPILOGUE

$\mathbb{D}$o our reformatories need reforming? That was the burnning question and critical issue in the mid 1950s that gave birth to a reform movement that was to challenge the Washington State Correctional System to its foundations and influence the shape of national prison policy for years to come. Dr. William Conte's painstaking and personal account of the era of reform revives and recreates the zeal of the reformers who sought to professionalize and humanize the administration of justice by implementing a modern treatment philosophy. It contrasts those efforts with the activities of others who sought to subvert and sabotage any departure from the traditional practices and policies. Dr. Conte has brought to life the age old question of how a society best deals with its deviant members and this work casts new light on many dark corners of recent correctional history.

This volume should prove to be a valuable reference not only for scholars and correctional professionals but also a useful resource for all those who care about the quality of justice in America now and in the future.

Norman Chamberlin
former Director, Pioneer Human Services
Consultant to an array of human services agencies and correctional programs

BIBLIOGRAPHY

Bain, W.F., Kimberling, D.A. The American Prison. American Correctional Association, 1983

Baker, J.E. The Right to Participate-Inmate Involvement in Prison Administration. The Scarecrow Press, Metuchen, N.J., 1974

Carter, Robert M., Glaser, Daniel, and Wilkins, Leslie T.T. Correctional Institutions. J.B. Lippincott Company, Philadelphia, N.Y., and Toronto, 1972

Clark, Richard X. (Edited by Leonard Levitt). The Brothers of Attica. Links Books, New York, 1973

Conte, William R. Modern Day Reforms in Washington State Penal Programs. American Journal of Corrections, May-June, p.3, 1971

Conte, William R. (Editor). Selected Writings of Garrett Heyns. The Sherwood Press, Olympia, 1974

Conte, William R., Sullivan, D.E., Johns, Donald R., Freeman, Robert A., Lizee, Robert P., Englund, Richard L., Gerecht, David. Selected Papers on Adult Corrections. The Bulletin (Department of Institutions), Vol XI, No. 1, March, 1970

Fenton, Norman. Human Relations in Adult Corrections. Charles C. Thomas, Springfield, Illinois, 1973

Graham, Gordon. The One-Eyed Man is King. Johnson Publishing Company, Loveland, 1982

Guiles, Fred Lawrence. Jane Fonda: The Actress In Her Time. Doubleday, Garden City, New York, 1982

Hagman, Tye. Reform 1957; A Skill, Recognition, A New Outlook. Perspective, Vol 1, No. 7, p.6, 1957

Heyns, Garrett. The Challenge of a Career in Corrections In a Changing Society. Manuscript, 1968

Manpower Needs: An Overview From An Institutions Director's Position. Read Before the WICHE Institute on Undergraduate Education For The Helping Institutions, Pocatello, Idaho, December 1965. Published: Biennial Report, Department of Institutions, 1968

Remarks of Doctor Garrett Heyns. Read Before The Institute On Correctional Manpower and Training. Alderbrook Inn, Union, Washington, April 2, 1965

The Road Ahead In Corrections. Federal Probation, Vol 33, No. 1, March, 1969

A Survey Of Adult Corrections. Read Before the Governors' Conference, Miami Beach, Florida, July 1963

The "Treat-'Em-Rough" Boys Are Here Again. Federal Probation, Vol 31, No. 2, June, 1967

Some Trends In Modern Penology. Manuscript. Date Unknown

Horney, Karen. The Neurotic Personality of Our Time. W.W. Norton, 1937

Killinger, George G., Cromwell, Paul F., Wood, Jerry M. Penology: The Evolution of Corrections in America. West Publishing, Saint Paul, Minnesota, 1979

McCoy, John and Hoffman, Ethan. The Concrete Mama. The University of Missouri Press, Columbia, 1981

Menninger, Karl. A Psychiatrist's World. The Viking Press, New York, 1959 (Part V: The Psychiatrist Afield)

Menninger, Karl. The Crime of Punishment. The Viking Press, New York, 1966

Mitford, Jessica. Kind and Usual Punishment. Alfred A. Knopf, New York, 1973

Planning Prospectus. (Adult Corrections). The Division of Institutions, State of Washington 1969

Redl, F. and Wineman, D. The Aggressive Child. The Free Press, Glencoe, Illinois, 1958

Transactions of the National Congress on Penitentiary and Reformatory Discipline (October 12-18, 1870). Published by The American Corrections Association, October, 1970

Rhay, B.J. Why Ex-Convicts Should Be Hired. Perspective, Vol 4, No. 5, p.5, May-June, 1960

Stastny, Charles and Tyrnauer, Gabrielle. Who Rules the Joint? Lexington Books, D.C. Heath and Company, Lexington, Massachusetts and Toronto, 1982

Tucker, Julia and Olsson, Barbara H. The American Prison. A Pictorial History. The American Correctional Association, 1978

Wicker, Tom. A Time To Die. Quadrangle/The New York Times Book Co., New York, 1975

Yochelson, Samuel. The Criminal Personality. Jason Aronson, New York, 1977

INDEX